To
My Mother
ALTAF JEHAN BEGUM

PREFACE

Khusro was born in India in 1252 AD as Abul Hasan Yameenuddin. His father, Amir Saifuddin, was a Turk from Central Asia and his mother an Indian Rajput, the daughter of the then Prime Minister, Amad ul Mulk. His father died when he was young, and he was brought up by his maternal grandfather in affluence. Both Amir and Khusro were his titles, of which Khusro he adopted as his pen name. During his lifetime he became a favorite of kings and princes and was loved by the great mystic, Khaja Nizamuddin Aulia of Delhi, India. He was buried next to him when he died at the age of 73 years in 1325 AD.

He grew up to be a great poet - musician of all times, with the magical qualities of Greek Orpheus. He invented several enduring musical instruments and wrote many famous ragas. Since his father spoke Turkish and Persian and his mother Hindi, he was fluent in all three and this helped him invent a new language - Urdu - which is a mixture of those three languages. It is now spoken by about four hundred million people in the world and is also the official language of Pakistan. He wrote profusely in Persian, Hindi and his new language, Urdu, but much of his writings has been lost, though part of his Persian poetry, mainly odes, among others has survived.

Translation by its very nature cannot capture the taste and flavor of the original. It is not possible to translate the beat, the rhythm and the flow of Khusro's odes in another language. However, I have tried to preserve some of these by translating his couplets as couplets.

Khusro is a romanticist par excellence. So like all romanticists, he loves feminine beauty and all the good things that go with it:

Everybody loves her lovely face
For it has beauty, charm and grace

Her lips are juicy, luscious, and red
Her kiss can revive even the dead

And the darling dimple of her dainty chin
If you don't kiss it, it would be a sin

It's nice to be in the park with girls
And smell the locks and play with curls

And try to look into their eyes
While they enchant and mesmerize

And tell them how you love their lips
Their necks and shoulders, their waists and hips
And if they resist and start to fight
Try to be gentle but hold them tight

And if they are stony hard and cold
Be not discouraged and try to be bold

And listen to KHUSRO and lose not heart
Even if you find them cruel and tart

He not only loves beautiful women but also their faults.
And when he describes these faults, he becomes delicious:

Oh, praise the Lord, the holy and pure, the maker of us all
For made He you from dust and clay a crafty, lovely doll

Cruel she is but don't call her that
Call her a lady though she is a brat

No one but her for me will do
Although she is a perfect shrew

I know a beauty who likes to boast
Of a beau to fry, and a lover to roast

He also advises us:

If she is yours because you are greedy
Better it is to be lonely and needy

And if she's yours because of your money
She is no honey, and it is not funny

And if she shows no mercy or pity
Delay you not and leave the city

And he uses his favorite *preacher to admonish us:*

When I fell in love, the preacher said
"She's a predator; you'll soon be dead

"You are a believer; she'll send you to hell
For she is a remorseless infidel

" Without her you will be in pain
And she will leave you again and again

"But you're in love; you've taken the bait
You must now KHUSRO resign to fate"

But then he yearns and craves for them and when he does,
he can make us cry:

Oh, how can I this rainy night without my darling sleep
When everyone is weeping here, weep I and clouds weep

Without you, darling, the gardens are in grip of doom and gloom
So shining brightly in the dark, my sweet sunshine, come to me

Lastly he also cannot help turning to God and become mystical:

To have a drink I went to the bar
And saw a mystic sitting not far

Half-drunk was he and half in trance
When he raised his eyes and flashed a glance

The maids of the bar were flirting with men
And the men were happy and saying amen

The candles were also burning very bright
And trying to dispel the dark of night

So after the mystic gave me a glance
He said hello while still in a trance

And asked me to come and sit by him
And fill my cup right up to the brim

And then he whispered this in my ear
"Love you always and love without fear"
And finally, with considerable relief, he ends:

And when I'm dying she'll say, "Gee whiz
What a hapless lover my KHUSRO is"

Khalid Hameed Shaida, MD
E Mail: khalmeed@aol.com
Web: www.writing.com/authors/khalmeed

1 Abr meebaarad o mun meeshawam az yaar juda

No, leave me not, my sweetie pie; enjoy this rainy day
And tear you not my love from this my loving heart away

Oh, how can I this rainy night without my darling sleep
When everyone is weeping here, weep I and clouds weep

With the air so fresh and clear, and the garden lush and green
Oh, why is not our nightingale a part of the lovely scene?

For you, my one and only one, I shed the tears of blood
So don't be out of my sight, for it will become a flood

O light you're of my eyes; O you're my gift of sight
And when you are away from me, my day looks more like night

I love to peek, and to ogle you from every chink and crack
My eyes will surely crack up, dear, if they not keep the track

Away not go from your KHUSRO lest you do start to whittle
Like a flower you're going to wither when cut you're from thistle

2 Sad hazaaraan aafreen jaanaafreen e paak ra

O praise the Lord, the holy and pure, the maker of us all
For made He you from dust and clay a crafty, lovely doll

So sweet and bitter, so tart and luscious, you can be all in one
Dispense you can a poison such, the cure for which is none

The soul you are of blossom, and you make the garden bloom
And when you go, you leave it in a deadly, deadly gloom

When out of sight you are, my love, my tears block my light
When wetter become my eyes yet, they whet my appetite

With magic in those eyes of yours oh, how you on me prey
So leave me not, O huntress, pray do not you go away

Comfort me not, O doctor; please sew not my wounded heart
For me to vent my longings all you let it fall apart

O cry not, KHUSRO, all the time your bitterness down you tone
For soften a heart a bit you can't when made it is of pure stone

3 Geh az mai talkh meekun aan do laal e shakkarafshaan ra

Well, if she makes her sweet lips tart with the wine just a trace
Keep that should all the oglers off staring at her face

Oft I reveal my love for her and hope that she will imbibe
Knowing well she loves me not, and takes she not a bribe

To soothe my lust I ask her oft for a kiss of her flaming cheek
The breath I use inflames my love; I get not what I seek

O burn me, God, instead of her in the fire of flaming hell
For knows she not the pain she gives; she really cannot tell

Tell, KHUSRO, the tale of Majno's love, and how endured he pain
For he was in love, and knew he not impatience how to rein

4 Beem ast keh sodayat, baigaana kunad ma ra

I fear my love for you, my love, will make me totally mad
And infamous so I'll become that it will make you sad

The passion I have will make me lose my reason and my creed
And the pangs will also make me reject my life and soul indeed

You have me bound, body and soul, with chains of braided hair
Now only you can make me free and get me off the snare

When sleep I can't, I drink and drink to drown my pain and sorrow
And drunk I get thinking of you when sober I'm next morrow

Like moon eclipsing a million stars, you eclipse the beauties all
And KHUSRO, like the moth, cannot resist your candle's call

5 Saba nau kard baagh o bostaan ra

In garden renewed by springtime breeze, its winter garment shed
The budding flowers like goblets wait for the vintage wine red

With gathering clouds in the heaven above letting water slowly drip
And birds all sing their melody sweet, like wine as rain they sip

The budding flowers, all ready to bloom, their lovely faces flush
With eager lips when kissed by birds, they blush, and blush, and blush

The oaks and pines are full and green with the advent of spring
And the songs of love by the loving birds make the lovely cypress swing

And when you arrive on such a scene with a smiling rosy face
I dare not say a rose you are, for you it might disgrace

So come, my love, and fill the cup with a lot of rosy wine
For time flies and the eternal life is neither yours nor mine

Be not so proud and learn you please, whatever you have, to savor
And don't you think the beauty you have will last somehow for ever

When KHUSRO comes to your salon, him you should try to reach
For find you will not a single one with such an eloquent speech

6 Chun bakshaaie lab e shakkarshikan ra

Open you when your sugary lips
Your word from them their sugar grips

And lit you have in my heart a fire
Which is consuming my being entire

And when in the garden you take a walk
Your beauty becomes its only talk

Excited, the birds run all amok
With envy the flowers go all in shock

But none of this affects your pride
Nor the stony heart that is inside

For the pain of KHUSRO there is no cure
The pangs of love even kings endure

3

7 Dar aamad dar dil aan sultaan e dilha

O beauty queen, come live in my heart
And make it your home; from it don't part

In it the seeds of love you sow
Then watch my terrible yearning grow

Take care of it and don't you throw
My poor little heart to the vulture and crow

Parting from you I can't endure
My sorrow and pain no one can cure

This love has set my heart on fire
And it is consuming my being entire

Your love from all does take its toll
And even our KHUSRO has lost his soul

8 Zahay wasf e labat zikr e zabaanha

Oh, how your lips are loved by all
And mouth also with pearls that fall

Your smile that makes you look like a flower
We love so much; we greatly admire

When heaven sees our flaming desire
Instead of a shower, it rains the fire

And when in the park, we cry with pain
The birds and the bees go all insane

And bleeding, when KHUSRO walks around
There're pools of blood all over the ground

9 Bashguft gulha dar chaman, aey gulsitaan e mun bia

Flowers are blooming everywhere, O flower of mine, come to me
Conifers await you night and day, my graceful pine, come to me

Thanks to my overflowing tears, tulips and roses are fresh and young
Strolling along the garden walk, my lily divine, come to me

Without you, darling, the gardens are in grip of doom and gloom
So shining brightly in the dark, my sweet sunshine, come to me

Your braids are trying to chain me, dear; your eyes are out to charm
So me if you want to captivate, my valentine, come to me

You may be tart and pungent but your absence is much worse
So bearing all your pungency, my vintage wine, come to me

Without you I, your KHUSRO, am tongue-tied and confused
To give me wit and fluency, O soul of mine, come to me

10 Gunj e ishq e to nihaan shud der dil e weeraan e ma

Smoldering is the fire of love in the wasteland of my heart
Consume it will my body and soul; my heart will fall apart

Leave me alone, O doctor, please, I feel completely sure
That she, who gave this pain to me, does also have the cure

Among the beauties of the world, you stand above and all alone
So be a queen and rule them all, and let them moan and groan

And when you come to walk in the park, they gossip and they talk
In charm and grace you are alone; no one can walk the way you walk

With you not there, your lovers are in agony and in pain
For deep in love these lovers are; do not them you disdain

They sob, they sigh, they weep, they cry, they moan all night, and groan
And even in a crowd, my dear, they feel all lonely, all alone

But lucky was KHUSRO when, with a wink, you said, "O I will be
His real love, his only love, but he will have to die for me"

11 Dar kham e gaisoo e kaafirkaish daari taarha

Lo, tangled are the pious ones in the curly brown hair
And caught is all their piety in its wavy, twisted snare

And dazzled so the learned are by the beauty of her face
That gone are all their tact and wit, and lost they have their grace

The clamors and the tumults are, of every shade and grade
The powers of the beauty and also its tools of trade

Yet kissing her lovely ruby lips is a pleasure and a thrill
A cure for every malady and a curb for every ill

The path of love and passion is a thorny one indeed
But follow will I the rose of mine, if she will take the lead

And I'll reach there even when it takes me years and years
If short of water the garden is, I'll supply it with my tears

So, KHUSRO, it is the long and short of the story of my love
And love is what it takes to keep the stars and moon in place above

12 Khabarat hast keh az khaish khaber neest mara

How numb am I you know not, dear
No hope have I, no qualm, no fear

Headlong in love, I have lost my head
Headless am I, neither live nor dead

Crying and weeping, having caused a flood
My eyes are dry, no tears, no blood

With bonds so strong no one can tear
Bound am I by her braided hair

Unable to win her stubborn streak
Surrendered have I to her strange mystique

And like a climber in quest of a peak
I am a moth, and a star I seek

Judging from, KHUSRO, her beautiful face
You have lost it all; you have no case

13 Her keh zaer e parahan beenad mara

Under my shirt you have to look to find the real me
And when you do, instead of me, a carcass you'll see

But even though half dead am I, that bad it cannot be
You might see some life in me, using my eyes when you see

Oh, would it not be wonderful if everyone could see
Me doing tete-a-tete with you over a cup of tea

So please, my love, be nice to me; you do not want to see
The crows and vultures eating me and people saying gee!

A lover great you may not be but wonder oft do we
If Romeo had to do, KHUSRO, what you've done, would he?

14 Aey, ba badi kerda baaz chashm e badaamoaz ra

Ruination wrought by your magical eyes
Even fate can't do, even if it tries

Happy are lovers with what they get
Obey they do and never regret

Be not so proud of beauty, my pet
What does not last, people forget

Life is short, and the time flies
Only death is sure and the rest are lies

So spend it all and leave no sum
Because tomorrow may never come

15 Noosheen labay keh laalash nau kard jaam e Jum ra

Those juicy lips with the ruby wine
Of which the kings for a sip do pine

Someone so nice giving so much pain
Sounds unreal and not very sane

Hungry they are but God they seek
Mystics are preys to her misty mystique

A losing lover knows what love is
Knows not the winner, for she is his

To no one we lovers can find to turn
We love, we hope, we wish, we yearn

And so is KHUSRO, the poor, the meek
Look, how love's made him frail and weak

16 Gufti zay dil baroon kun ghamha e baikaraan ra

Come, O my love and ease the pain
Promise I do I'll never complain

Since you, O robber, took my heart
Sleep I cannot; I'm falling apart

Without you, nights are dark and long
So come, my love, to where you belong

With tossing and turning all night in bed
It is a wonder that I am still not dead

My bleeding heart turns everything red
And blood is what my eyes shed

With sigh and gasp, when I respire
I breathe not smoke but also fire

And when in the garden I see a rose
Oh, how I miss you, God only knows

Without you, darling, as KHUSRO knows
Night and day my sorrow grows

17 Shafa'at aamadam aey dost deeda e khud ra

Keep him not waiting, my girl, anymore
His soul is aching; his heart is sore

Half dead already and quite insane
Dying he is of sorrow and pain

With agony and pain he's crying, my dear
Be kind to him, and give him your ear

With sorrow and pain going on and on
Worn out he is, and his patience gone

His longing and yearning have set him on fire
And captive he is of his burning desire

Burning he is, and his condition is dire
Consumed has passion his being entire

So it's the story of KHUSRO'S desire
What'll happen to him, do not inquire!

18 Shanaakht aan keh gham o mehnat e judaaie ra

He who knows separation and pain
Should he not from love refrain?

Oh, no one wants his girl to leave
But what if fate wants her to cleave?

Her face reflected in the beauty of moon
And shine it does like sun in June

If she is yours because you're greedy
Better it is to be lonely and needy

And if she's yours because of your money
She is no honey, and it's not funny

And if she shows no mercy or pity
Delay you not and leave the city

So go to the bar, and do thank God
It's better to be bad than be a fraud

And love, O KHUSRO, if love you must
And bite the dust but don't ever lust

19 Guzisht umr o hunooz az taqallub o soada

Though weak and old, I love you still
And wait and wait though hope is nil

I wait and watch, and watch and wait
And tell myself it's never too late

Loving with all my heart, O mate
I cannot help for it's my fate

Feeling very sorry, to the pub I go
There in a cup I drown my woe

And there I find my peace and ease
My pain and woe at the bar all cease

But in the morn, when sober again
Return my sorrow, grief, and pain

Then evening comes and I adjourn
To the bar again and take my turn

But great it is in love to fall
O KHUSRO, because it conquers all

20 Aey baad, burqa barfigan aan roo e aatishnaak ra

Hide you not your lovely face, O love, behind the veil
And let their eyes feast a little, for lovers are weak and frail

Shedding they are the tears of blood for you, O cruel one
Better to die than have some hope when there is really none

Covered they are with blood, my dear, they have no hopes, no fears
To wash the blood from everywhere it takes a flood of tears

You tell those lovely eyes of yours, they not bind the spell
No noose you need for the hapless ones, your curly hair you tell

And walk you not in tight skirt, showing all those lovely curves
It does not serve the lovers well, and it's not good for nerves

And handle KHUSRO with utmost care, for his condition is dire
A spark is all it takes, my dear, to set his heart on fire

21   Aey shehsawaar, narmtarak raan samand ra

Your ladyship, ride not so rough in the infantry of lovers
For they are seasoned worshipers; they are no amateurs

You are like the cypress tree, so tall, so slim, so trim
So when they try to look at you, do not you be so grim

Your eyes are full of mystical flair; your curly hair a snare
But if they want to sit and stare, don't tell them—don't you dare!

And do not try advising them and tell them to go away
For they're in love, and counsel such will have on them no sway

And KHUSRO is, like the rest of them, so much in love with you
So hurt him not you anymore when next he comes to woo

22   Aawurda am shafi e dil e zaar e khaish ra

My wounded heart, oh, how it cries
Do teach some pity to your cruel eyes

Delicate you are, I would rather die
Than give you my burden, and make you cry

He makes me jealous who looks at you
I envy sometimes my own eyes, too

Free is the man who, without strife
Frees at your feet his captive life

Down I am but with all due grace
I'll hold up my head to see your face

If you can't be sweet, be bitter and tart
But ignore you not my wounded heart

Your KHUSRO is dying, but before he dies
Do train on him your deadly eyes

23 Bashgaaft gham een jaan e jigarekhaara e ma ra

This all-consuming, burning desire
Oh, how it devours my being entire

There is no cure for a broken heart
Part by part, it is falling apart

O morning breeze, when there you go
Do find my heart and say hello

And if you see her, give her a kiss
Tell her how badly her company I miss

And ask if she does why I'm not dead
Say life I cannot without her shed

Tell her, without her, my condition is dire
My burning desire has my heart on fire

And say to KHUSRO that love is tricky
And a lot more difficult if one is so picky

24 Baroo, aey baad, o paish e deegraan deh jalwa bustaan ra

O breeze of spring, blow not so loud
Without my cypress, don't be so proud

Hurry up, O doctor, my wounds you sew
For she will be sorry if she comes to know

I am ready to die whenever she says
For all I need is her magical gaze

And ask not about my sorrowful soul
It is no use, and don't you console

Teach not her eyes any compassion
Let them practice their naked aggression

Talk not of freedom, he does not care
For KHUSRO is happy bound by her hair

25 Burqa barafgan, aey pari, husn e bala'angaaiz ra

Come lift the veil, O splendid one, and let them see your face
And dazzle them all with charm and wit, and show them all your grace

And let your golden locks and curls fly freely in the air
And fill the world with fragrance of your lovely curly hair

Look, all these men oh, how they flock to catch a glimpse of you
And how they fall and die for you when trying their best to woo

And some of them, who do not die, are only half alive
And they're in such a poor shape, them doctors won't revive

Your KHUSRO is also miserable, shedding his blood in tears
He wants from you much sympathy; he needs a lot of cheers

26 Behr e to khalqay meekushad
aakhir mun e badnaam ra

Oh, what do I do with my crazy heart?
It's been my trouble from the very start

When in the terrace she appears like moon
My heart goes wild; I begin to croon

And when she holds the cup to her lip
On my foolish old heart I lose my grip

When her curly hair flies in the air
My heart can't bear; it feels despair

And when she rouges her rosy cheek
Inflames she my heart; it begins to shriek

With all this, my heart drives me to brink
I rush to the bar and drink and drink

O KHUSRO, your troubles are no one's fault
What does your fate, no one can halt

27   Chun der chaman rawi, az khanda lab mabund aan ja

When in the garden, do smile, my dear
Don't give the flowers a chance to sneer

Many a preacher thinks love is a vice
I have no use for such an advice

To reach your balcony, no one tries
It's so high, there the sun can't rise

Braid your hair and make a chain
Because your lovers are all insane

To catch your lovers, you make the snare
Of your golden tresses and curly hair

And keep them all as captives there
Lest them it stirs, keep out the air

Be nice to KHUSRO; he is also not free
And there's no one more miserable than he

28   Chun khaahi burd roozay aaqibat een jaan e maftoon ra

On the Day of Judgment, I'll not rise
Unless you came in an angel's guise

And I won't bother your palace guard
Kissing the gate will be my reward

But I can't help if my tears of blood
Reveal my secrets by causing a flood

At night, when I think of my day with you
My flaming heart gives me the cue

In the dark of night when you aren't there
I can't help thinking of the black, curly hair

And when I discover that I'm not free
I thank my star; I am filled with glee

I do not mind my bleeding heart
What's hard to take is my rival's dart

With words, O KHUSRO, you can bind a spell
But charming a charmer, you can't do well

14

29 Dilam der aashiqi aawaara shud awaarater baada

If vagrancy is love's reward, so be it
If sadness is also love's award, so be it

Her hair does plunder your peace of mind
If you against it cannot guard, so be it

Her lovely face is full of grace
If her heart is also stony hard, so be it

Says preacher, madness is part of love
But if it cannot you retard, so be it

Her eyes are cruel but full of charm
If trump they your every card, so be it

Her gaze can shatter a heart to pieces
And if it hits you like a shard, so be it

Your love is, KHUSRO, full of tears
But if it's your only reward, so be it

30 Gercheh barbood aql o deen e mara

Though she plundered my faith, my reason
It's only a game; it is no treason

Her ears are covered with precious stones
She cannot hear my moans and groans

Your park has cypress, and oak, and pine
But where, O gardener, is my conifer divine

I do not mind if she breaks my heart
But take I cannot my rival's dart

For you, O preacher, it's a silly emotion
But deserves my idol my love, my devotion

O cry not, KHUSRO, you might drown
In the flood of tears the entire town

31 Deewaana kard zulf e to dar yak nazar mara

One look from you and I'm crazy about you
And your braided hair, it has chained me, too

Your stony heart is hard like a rock
It breaks my heart like a fragile crock

I would love to kiss your juicy red lip
And drink its wine only sip by sip

Your lips are sugar, your face a flower
But together, my love, they can be sour

You are my soul, my heart, my life
But then you're also a dagger, a knife

So come to KHUSRO, though not a king
He writes verses and can also sing

32 Saaqia, paish aar jaam e baa safa e khaish ra

O come, my love, and fill the cup with the vintage ruby wine
In a way that I can see in it your reflection divine

When you hold the cup in your ivory hand, it does reflect your face
And pull it does from everywhere the men of every race

Leisurely walking in the park when you step in a flower bed
The tulip and rose cling to your feet, and paint your toenails red

And when in the garden, the roses there see you with rosy cheek
Afford they cannot to be so proud, so nightingales they seek

O morning breeze, to the park you go and do some fragrance bring
The winter days are finally gone, so let's enjoy the first of spring

So come, my love, and fill the cup with the vintage ruby wine
In a way that I can see in it your reflection divine

33 Bus keh ander dil faroburdam hawa e neesh ra

Her gaze, like a dart, when it hits my heart
The fire of love does it there start

A home for love when God couldn't find
He turned to the heart of the humankind

Anyone who knows not the aching heart
He hasn't been hit by her eye's dart

No lance, no arrow she needs to kill
She uses her eyes with great skill

O preacher, be wary, it'll burn you entire
By blaming my heart, you're playing with fire

To look at your rival don't, KHUSRO, try
Oh, he is so ugly you will hurt your eye

34 Bahaar aamad o sabza nau shud ba jooha

The spring has come, and green are the dales
And the garden's brides have dropped their veils

With goblets in hands the tulips do wait
To get their share from the wine pails

The flowers are blooming with buds in their wake
But the poor little blue bird, he only wails

Walking near water are beauties in gowns
On the arms of men dressed up in tails

The tulips and roses are impudent and saucy
And laughing at lovers are the nightingales

And the flowers, hearing the verses of KHUSRO
Are spreading their scent in meadows and vales

17

35 Baashad aan rozay keh beenam ghamgusaar e khaish ra

If I could only share my pain
With someone friendly and humane

If only had I not to wait
And wait, and wait, and be irate

If only I had some access
To my lovely cypress, and to caress

If I could find my lovely girl
Better than any gem or pearl

I'd not have to drown my sorrow
In a cup of wine night and morrow

So bring the serpents of her curls
To guard my heart with gems and pearls

36 Aey, bai to gulha e chaman shusta ba khoon rukhsaarha

Without you blood in tears they shed
And make the flowers their beds all red

And I have also become very frail
I've lost my color; my cheeks are pale

Without you, darling, I would rather be dead
In the game of love, I've staked my head

I cry and cry so much with pain
No blood in me will soon remain

And also, using your eye's dart
You have wounded my woeful heart

A total loser was KHUSRO born
He wants a rose but gets a thorn

37 Shabay deedam chu meh ber baam o ra

Her in her terrace I saw last night
Sitting and drinking in the cool moonlight

Hoping and praying that when she'll see
She'll say something rather nice to me

And even if something she said very bad
Just getting her attention I will be glad

A person who falls in love with her
He should not mind from her a slur

And anyone who falls for her curly hair
Mind he shouldn't being caught in a snare

And a man who wants to kiss her feet
He finds that it is quite a treat

But whenever to her KHUSRO she tries to be nice
His fate extracts from him the price

38 Rooz e eid ast, ba mun deh mai e naabay chu gulaab

Finished is fasting, pour me the wine
Infuse some life in the carcass of mine

Let not the life from my body flee
This pain of parting is killing me

See now, the people who used to fast
Without the wine they cannot last

And those to the mosque who used to go
Now in the bar they nightly show

And those who wouldn't sing and dance
Now they would never miss a chance

And the barmaid too does a nice job
With the wine she now serves kabob

In short, it's time to eat and drink
And about the rest let's not think

39 Zaad chun az subh e roshan aaftaab

Look, my love, at the glorious dawn
And give me wine before it is gone

Blessed is he who is always drunk
And has his woes in the wine sunk

Piety and love you just can't mix
Like water and liquor when a drink you fix

I know a beauty who likes to boast
Of a beau to fry, and a lover to roast

I wish one night she, in my dream
Will kiss my mouth before I scream

Oh, how her ear, which her tresses shroud
Looks like the sun behind a cloud

The barmaid was nice; she held back nothing
So all night we drank and toasted the king

40 Zahay namood az aan zulf o aariz o rukh e khoob

Her locks, and cheeks, and a lovely face
Are snakes, and roses, and a charming grace

They all so heavily weigh on my heart
Being hard, and painful, and very, very tart

Despite it all we need not fear
They're also friendly, tender, and dear

But by their nature, they're mighty rude
And strong, and pushy, and very crude

And they can be also good in stealth
By bringing pleasure, health, and wealth

Beyond it all that's mentioned above
They're the objects of passion and love

It's all true, KHUSRO, but let's not think
And go to the bar, and have a drink

41 Ager ba goashanasheenaan numayad aan rukh e khoob

If to the mystics she shows her face
She makes them lose the divine grace

A lot of trouble are her lovely eyes
All sorts of charms they can devise

And when she leaves, we feel the pain
Which can drive us all insane

When she's away, she writes a note
To make us feel even more remote

And she can set our hearts on fire
And burn our bodies and souls entire

But, KHUSRO, for you it's beyond control
She rules your heart and owns your soul

42 Imshab shab e mun noor zay mehtaab e digger daasht

Tonight I see a different moon
The singers have also a new tune

People are going to the mosque to pray
But the idol of mine I'll never betray

With her gaze a dagger and lash a knife
For her charming eyes I'll give my life

Her sleepy eyes do keep me awake
The spell they cast I cannot break

By a million knots, I'm bound to her curls
And she keeps adding more knots and swirls

Of life in KHUSRO there is no sign
Since he has been drinking this new wine

43 Taqdeer keh yak chand mara az to juda daasht

Though fate has kept me away from you
I blame my life for not saying adieu

The pain of parting they only know
Who've seen their loves forever go

I'm not sorry for losing my life
I wish my blood hadn't soiled your knife

When a mystic sees you strolling in the park
His quest for the Divine goes off the mark

Gave life your KHUSRO for you because
More loyal to you than your dog he was

44 Afsoes az een umr keh berbaad e hawa raft

Oh, how this love has ruined my life
It's all sorrow, pain, and strife

You're at the height of youth and beauty
We do your bidding as a matter of duty

From the world of woes it's a retreat
Don't drive me out of your street

Oh, this waiting and waiting is a burden great
To be relieved of it I cannot wait

Losing my life I do not dread
In the game of love, I've staked my head

With poise, O KHUSRO, you must proceed
For patience is what in love you need

45   Dilay kash sabr nabwad aan e mun neest

The patience in love is not for me
To part with her I cannot agree

My tale of love you might recall
Has no forbearance in it at all

The heart that she has set on fire
A flood of tears it does require

O tearful eyes, don't you cry
Putting out the fire don't even try

From wisdom when I asked advice
Said it, for a lover it won't suffice

I showed my gal when my bleeding heart
She smiled and said, "It's not my dart

"It's no use, KHUSRO, do not cry
No one cares if you live or die"

46   Zay mun naazukmiaanay dour maandaast

My gal has left and gone away
My life is much in disarray

My heart is heavy; my life bleak
I'm so weak I can hardly speak

My cries of pain, oh, no one hears
I weep and shed my blood in tears

My pain and sorrow he only knows
Who has been in love and knows its woes

And I am like a nightingale
Without the rose, who can only wail

From place to place I rove and roam
Like a stranger who has lost his home

O breeze, you go to her and tell
Without her KHUSRO'S life is hell

47   Dil e miskeen e mun der band maandaast

My poor little heart, it's her slave
For a lovely smile it does so crave

With so much pain it's short of space
For counsel my heart doesn't have a place

But please, O preacher, for me do pray
For she is the eagle, and I'm the prey

With love to her I was firmly bound
And the bond remains when she isn't around

From the world of woe it's my retreat
So please not drive me out of her street

For the love of God, give me some wine
To quench, O barmaid, this thirst of mine

And you can hurt his feelings again and again
For KHUSRO'S happy with sorrow and pain

48   Nigaara, chu to zaeba kas nadeedaast

No one is more beautiful than you
Your charm and grace have very few

O come and dazzle us all today
Until tomorrow please not delay

So come and show us your lovely face
Your charming bloom, your glorious grace

My tears betrayed my love for you
Their sudden surge I couldn't subdue

Oh, tell me not to restrain my zeal
You should know me and how I feel

But if you do not like his role
Give KHUSRO back the heart you stole

49 Mara waqtay dilay azaad boodast

There was a time my heart was free
And it was full of mirth and glee

There was a time my heart was wise
My wit and reason were all with me

O please, my love, don't be so cruel
And hear your lover's earnest plea

If scent of your hair were not in the air
I wouldn't have lost my sanity

And if my life were in my sighs
It would've been easy for it to flee

Fret not, KHUSRO, about your fate
You'll feel better; just look at me

50 Saba garday az aan zulf e do ta khaast

When your curly locks fly in the air
The scent of your hair goes everywhere

The flowers in bloom start to blush
And your lovers also feel the flush

To your lovers do please be kind
For being in love, they're in a bind

The fire of love they cannot control
And it's consuming their heart and soul

Being trapped and caught in a deadly snare
They are the captives of your curly hair

And seeing its beauty, and charm, and grace
Dazzled they are by your lovely face

And if you are fond of seeing the shows
Come and see KHUSRO with all his woes

51 Mun o shab, zindagaani e mun een ast

Pain and sorrow, woe and strife
Day and night all my life

A tearful eye, a bleeding heart
Gave me she and did depart

The parting pain and nights dark
On this life I now embark

Wait and hope, and hope and wait
It's my business; it's my fate

I die and live, and live and die
And in between, I cry and cry

I'll lay my life at her feet
And then my job will be complete

But, KHUSRO, I'll remain her slave
Until I end up in my grave

52 Mara der sar hawa e naazneenayast

I am in love with a beautiful lass
Who took my wit and faith alas

She will be never out of my heart
Though she is breaking it all apart

Everyone loves her curly hair
Be it a pauper or a billionaire

I wish one day she'll step on my grave
And a print of her foot on it engrave

From it will grow the flowers in spring
And no one will have to bring anything

And one day from it will Narcissus arise
To remind me of her enchanting eyes

So ever since Cupid has KHUSRO hit
He has lost his reason, faith, and wit

53 Nigaara, rooz e aish o shaadmaaniest

My love, it's time to drink and eat
And sing, and dance, and feast, and treat

Except you, darling, I have no one
My life is dull; no joy, no fun

Nothing in the world can hypnotize
Like your charming, dreamy eyes

Your every curl is like bait
To trap and snare and captivate

My love, your lashes are like darts
They hit, they jab, they wound the hearts

But you're a friend of all but me
And I've no friend but my agony

So be nice to KHUSRO, for he is sweet
And listening to him is a real treat

54 Nagooyam dar to aibay, aey pisar, hast

Although, my darling, you are perfect
Fidelity from you I cannot expect

When you're gone, I cannot sleep
And in your absence, I weep and weep

Since I've been hit by your eye's dart
I've been nursing a wounded heart

Though I miss you, and cry and cry
Your image does never leave my eye

When not in love, I had no woe
But now to love my life I owe

Your rosy cheek is one of a kind
It's something in Heaven you cannot find

My heart you wanted; I gave it to you
And I'll do whatever you want me to do

Says KHUSRO, dark is the parting night
With the end of the tunnel having no light

55 Jafa kaz way bar een jaan e zaboon raft

Her cruel eyes will take my life
To shed my blood she needs no knife

I saw her once, and through my eyes
She went to the heart and got her prize

And as she came, my life fled
In love I'm neither alive nor dead

Telling my tale of love I dread
For blood in tears do people shed

The picture of pain so well I paint
That before I finish, they start to faint

My tale but, KHUSRO, to her don't tell
Charming a charmer, I can't do well

56 Bia aey, deeda e shehray ba sooyat

Looking they go from place to place
They all want to see your lovely face

Your eyes cause a lot of woe
They wound and kill wherever they go

And even a mirror in which you look
You fill with terror its every nook

For a kiss my plea when you dismiss
The paw of your dog I go and kiss

Someday, my love, do grant my plea
Don't always tell me, "O don't be silly"

Much like a bee around a rose
I would love to be around you close

Like KHUSRO I rehearse around the clock
But when I see you I cannot talk

57   Ishq e to bala e jaan basand ast

Though this love is killing me
Her smiling face is a source of glee

With those lovely, enchanting eyes
Everyone she can mesmerize

The deadly bow of her lovely brow
Escaping a prey, it doesn't allow

But bait and trap she does not use
With a wink, her prey she can seduce

For my crazy heart whenever I look
I find she has it on her deadly hook

O fate of mine, do let me go
I do not need another woe

And someone other than KHUSRO seek
For this love has made him so very weak

58   Mai noesh keh dour e shaadmaaniest

The times are good, so let's all drink
From having fun we shouldn't shrink

Let's all in wine put our trust
For in the end, we'll all be dust

And one day surely without fuss
The bell is going to toll for us

So let's enjoy our girls and wine
And let's go out, and drink, and dine

Half dead we are and half alive
Let's with wine our hearts revive

Being in love, we cannot sleep
We're like dogs and watch we keep

And in boasting, KHUSRO, let's not wallow
For the drums we beat are so very hollow

59 Baaz, jaanaan, aatish e shouq e to dar jaan ja garift

When love in us ignites the fire
We lose our heads and gain desire

And when in trance, she begins to dance
Our hearts and minds don't have a chance

And soon a spark within the breast
Engulfs the heart and all the rest

But we, ignoring the preacher's advice
With the idols of ours, are in paradise

Anyone who loves with heart and soul
In Heaven and Earth attains his goal

And, KHUSRO, there's no greater treat
Than being with the dogs in her street

60 Chun ba geeti hercheh meeaayad rawaan khahadguzisht

This life is short, O don't you know?
So do some good before you go

See, how the pomp of a mighty king
All goes unto dust like everything

Knowing how fickle is the world of ours
We are so lured by its ugly powers

But even those so mighty and august
Do lie in the dust as all things must

And be it winter or be it spring
It too shall pass like anything

Beware, O KHUSRO, of the worldly things
They come attached with terrible strings

61 Baa ghamash khoo kardam, imshab gercheh dar zaari guzisht

Last night I cried and cried and cried
I missed her so much I almost died

The memory kept me awake all night
Of nights with her in the full moonlight

I also remembered the beautiful treat
When I could sleep in her busy street

And then I thought of her lovely snare
When caught I was in her curly hair

There was a time when I was cool
I was a fool but a wise fool

Now with my rival when she spends the night
I cannot sleep; I am so uptight

My life, O KHUSRO, is full of sorrow
At night I feel there'll be no morrow

62 Chun guzar bar khaak daari, bar sarat een baad cheest

The life is fickle; don't be so proud
If proud you must be, don't be so loud

If fate is bad, blame not the star
Accuse the driver and not the car

Of telling truth don't be afraid
If it's a spade, call it a spade

Love has both joy and pain
So you neither rave nor complain

Nothing is worse than greed and lust
Yourself you blame, and blame you must

With a captive soul, you can't be free
With pain in the heart, you can't have glee

O KHUSRO, your sorrow do not disclose
Burden her not with your dreadful woes

63 Yaar ager bargasht, dar teemaar boodan hum khush ast

If she comes not, do not pout
If no doctor, you do without

If your love respects you not
On you, her lover, it's no blot

And if she always fights with you
It is for a lover nothing new

And if you cannot sleep with her
To her wishes you should defer

Love your idols but do not tell
For the sheik will call you an infidel

Among the preachers, be like a monk
And when in the bar, get always drunk

With her, O KHUSRO, if you cannot be
Don't lose your head and sanity

64 Yaar dil bardaasht waz ranj e dil e ma gham nadaasht

You took my heart and gave me pain
This love is driving me insane

Affected you aren't by my moan and groan
Though melt they can even a stone

My cry of pain is heard everywhere
But you ignore it and do not care

In your absence, I cry and cry
We are strangers, my patience and I

My love, I love my sorrow and pain
I promise that I will never complain

My ill, says KHUSRO, is beyond cure
What I cannot cure I must endure

65 Raft yaar o aarzoo e o zay jaan e mun naraft

She went but didn't spare my heart
Her image didn't from my eye depart

When I to the wild go in despair
My tears with me go everywhere

She kills and kills with her cruel eyes
And she would never apologize

Having lost my heart, I look everywhere
But where it is, I can't go there

So weak and frail, my love, I've grown
That feel it I in my every bone

My fire, O KHUSRO, has burnt his wing
So the bird her message cannot bring

66 Aan sawaar e kajkuleh kaz naaz sultaan e mun ast

The stylish lady is my queen
Her love has made me weak and lean

With her, my home is paradise
Her parting but is the devil's device

In her absence, I cry and cry
I moan, and groan, and sob, and sigh

To the wild I go in great despair
To me what happens I do not care

The rot I'm in I cannot halt
But if I'm wretched, it's my fault

And yet in spite of everything
Because I love, I feel like a king

And, KHUSRO, when I write my verse
I do it for the queen of my universe

67 Sarv e bustaan e malaahat, qaamat e raana e tust

Like cypress she is slim and trim
Without her light, my vision is dim

Wherever she goes, she makes a stir
Everyone is madly in love with her

The stars and moon, she makes them bright
She is the source of all their light

Whether in temple, mosque, or church
I see her wherever I go and search

To everyone joy and glee she brings
Her slaves she makes even the kings

To her when KHUSRO tells his sorrow
She always says, "Tell me tomorrow"

68 Khurram aan chashmay keh her roozash nazar bar roo e tust

Blessed is he who lives with her, and sees her everyday
And smells her lovely locks and curls, and with them does he play

Without her, I'm so miserable, and she has so much fun
She eats and drinks with one and all, and dances with everyone

Black her locks and tresses are; her curls are dark as night
Her lips are like the ruby wine; like moon her face is bright

With sugary lips and rosy cheeks and black enchanting eyes
She can directly cast a spell and easily hypnotize

Her brow is like a deadly bow; her gaze is like a dart
She can gash the strongest chest and easily wound a heart

Being fried or roasted or burned alive KHUSRO does not dread
But since he is a Muslim Turk, pray do not burn him dead

69 Ta khayaal e nuqta e khaalat sawaad e chashm e maast

Her mole is the apple of my eager eye
On the dirt of her feet my face rub I

The dust I take and put in my eye
From the road on which she rides by

The flowers in the park her lovers don't seek
Because they've seen her rosy cheek

To the mosque they do not go to pray
The arch of her brow now worship they

Having seen the twists and turns of her hair
They now feel trapped in its lovely snare

What kind of drinks, O barman, you make?
Everyone in the pub is wide awake

And without the barmaid's lovely face
KHUSRO in the bar feels out of place

70 Saaqia, mai deh keh imroozam sav e deewaangiest

Come, fill the cup; I need some glee
My empty cup is killing me

And if I'm dying, pity me not
Though pity a lover does need a lot

Burning, the moth makes a candle bright
Being burnt alive is the moth's delight

An amulet, preacher, I do not need
My monstrous love it'll only feed

My tale of love to my luck I tell
Hoping my gal wouldn't say farewell

My odes have all a crazy flair
I need the chain of her braided hair

A brazen lover does love the pain
You can't go crazy without a brain

So if she burns you, don't complain
And ask her, KHUSRO, to do it again

71 Khaana am weeraan shud az soada e khoobaan aaqibat

The love of beauties is killing me
My heart's in constant agony

My head that I used to hold so high
On their beautiful feet it does now lie

If a beauty wants to take my life
I'll gladly provide her with a knife

And though these women aren't very kind
In my heart a home they'll always find

They put me often in a terrible bind
But I love them, and I do not mind

My love for them I cannot resist
No matter what, it'll always persist

These beauties, KHUSRO, don't care a bit
Their love is deadly; I'll die of it

72 Dar shab e hijr keh az rooz e qayaamat batar ast

Without her the night is full of gloom
And the day is worse than the Day of Doom

The fire of love, without a doubt
With all your tears you can't put out

Her rosy cheek do the flowers envy
Her smile is sweet as sweet can be

O breeze, when you go to her street
Tell her I love her but do be discreet

The lover, though he doesn't know
His journey of love is full of woe

Though the preacher doesn't like it a bit
I love her too much; I'll never quit

He does not also like the wine
But KHUSRO thinks it is benign

73 Fitna e ahl e nazar chun ba jahaan tal'at e oast

Though it is charming and full of grace
A source of trouble is also her face

Although she drives me up the tree
A blessing she also happens to be

Poised and elegant also is she
She's tall and slim as a cypress tree

A lover wants to please the Lord
But the preacher needs to get his reward

When I'm confused, to the bar I go
To consult the barman, a real pro

When KHUSRO wants to feel upbeat
He goes and kisses the barmaid's feet

74 Band e jaanam zay kham e silsila e moo e kasayst

My soul is the captive of her curly hair
My heart is caught in its deadly snare

She gives me nothing but sorrow and pain
But favors my rival again and again

You must have gone to her house, O air
I smell her scent in you everywhere

O preacher, do not waste your advice
To have her, I will pay any price

Such a hold she has on me, I swear
Wherever I go, I see her there

Her spell on me I cannot disguise
I'm a slave of her enchanting eyes

Affection for KHUSRO she never displays
Although for her he always prays

75 Kushta e taigh e jafayat dil e durwaish e mun ast

My heart is a victim of her cruel eyes
They jab it with darts, and terrorize

Anyone who tells me to love her not
For him I do not care a lot

A belief I have, O preacher, indeed
My faith is love, and passion creed

For love and passion I have a knack
It's the patience that I sadly lack

Her sugary lips I love to kiss
A chance if I get, I rarely miss

Whenever she wants to get my heart
Gladly from me it does depart

But, KHUSRO, beware of her cruel eyes
Enchant they do and mesmerize

76 Ishq baa jaan baham az seena baroon khahad raft

When love decides your life to take
No charm or magic will give you a break

It needs no bribe, no lure, no bait
Your heart and soul to captivate

It can also with a wink revive
Whether you're dead or half alive

From eyes and heart when it makes you bleed
Wherever you look, there is blood indeed

And when your rival you see succeed
It makes, not eyes, but your soul bleed

So love from your heart you cannot erase
Especially, KHUSRO, when you see her face

77 Ta nadaani zay dilam yaar baroon khahad raft

My heart this love will never leave
Nothing will ever my agony relieve

My Turko girl, she wounds me so
And yet my life wouldn't leave me and go

Drunk when she goes out in the street
Seeing her walking is a real treat

From eyes her image does not part
And when it does, it goes to the heart

The pang of love that I've in my heart
Unto death it will never, never part

Of love no magic can dispel the pain
Your verses, O KHUSRO, you try in vain

78 Doash laal e to mara ta ba saher mehmaan daasht

Whenever she comes and sits by me
She instantly cures my agony

Her happy face dispels my pain
Though wounds in my heart still remain

When an order from her does a courier bring
It makes me feel that I am a king

Whenever she goes, I feel morose
But her longing stays and never goes

An idol, O preacher, if I adore
She is my goddess; you shouldn't deplore

If me she coyly ever sees
She does it only my rival to tease

Her affection KHUSRO does not crave
He is just happy being her slave

79 Ta zi'ad banda gham e ishq ba jaan khahad dasht

The pang of love is a part of life
With sorrow and pain my life is rife

Be kind to me, and never say never
Your youth and beauty won't last forever

The bow and arrow of your brow and gaze
Make hearts of lovers their favorite preys

You have repented, or so they say
I wish I could believe and say hurray

You, my love, I cannot forget
Having loved and lost, I don't regret

I know you wish that no one knew
Hide I cannot but my love for you

It's something, KHUSRO, you cannot fix
Passion and patience don't ever mix

80 Saaqia, baada deh imrooz keh jaanaan een jaast

Oh, give me some wine that she is here
It's a wonderful atmosphere

Though with her lips on which to feed
A wine sweet I should not need

And don't you cry, O nightingale
My rose is here without her veil

Don't let me die; do keep me alive
Now that she's here, I'll revive

O Angel of Death, don't interfere
She's my life and she's now here

Come see, O bee, her luscious lips
And how from them the honey drips

Looking for your heart? Look in her hair
KHUSRO, it's trapped in its deadly snare

81 Ger bagooyam keh daroon e dil e mun pinhaan cheest

In my heart please don't look
For there's sorrow in every nook

And if you want to take my life
Here's my heart, and here's the knife

My eyes have tears and my heart desire
And I am between the flood and fire

The flood of Noah my tears excel
My fire's the envy of the fire of hell

Without her help oh, I am stuck
I've been abandoned by my lady luck

If you don't believe me, ask your hair
How KHUSRO is doing as a captive there

82 Aan keh burdast dilam zulf e pareeshaan een ast

Caught in her curls is my poor heart
I've been wounded by her eye's dart

I hope she'll someday come to my grave
For even there, for her I'll crave

When I fell in love, the preacher said
"She's a predator; you'll soon be dead

"You're a believer; she'll send you to hell
For she is a remorseless infidel

"Without her you will be in pain
And she'll leave you again and again

"But you're in love; you've taken the bait
You must now, KHUSRO, resign to fate"

83 Ya Rab, ander dil e khaak aan gul e khandaan chun ast

Why is my flower in the dust so soon?
What happened, O God, to my shining moon?

I cry like Jacob day and night
Without my Joseph, I've lost my sight

Having lost all hope, in total despair
Looking for her, I go everywhere

Where did she go, my beautiful girl
My shining gem, my precious pearl?

My smiling flower, lovely and sound
Lies now deep under the ground

A fountain of youth, and life's spring
Look, how to death she does now cling

O what do I tell the people who say,
"Don't cry so much, O KHUSRO, pray"?

84 Dar saram ta zay sar e zulf e to soadaay hast

I'm crazy about her curly hair
In beauty and charm it's beyond compare

Oh, how her locks my heart steal
And how very nice they make it feel

The flowers, when they see her face
It makes them feel so commonplace

Without her, nights are long and dark
Desolate and lonely, bleak and stark

She is so tall, and slim, and trim
She makes the cypress look very grim

In her absence, I feel so sad
But cares she not, which makes me mad

Endure your pain, says KHUSRO, with grace
And look at her beautiful, radiant face

85 Sitamay az to kashad merd, sitam natwaan guft

Cruel she is but don't call her that
Call her a lady though she's a brat

No one but her for me will do
Although she is a perfect shrew

Her beauty is a foe of creed and reason
Her pride is beyond any comparison

The kings and princes she treats like dirt
She knows your feelings how to hurt

With her, so proud, and rude, and vain
Trying to reason is totally insane

If me someday she would like to kill
I'll let her, KHUSRO, O yes, I will

86 Asaray namaand baaqi zay mun ander aarzooyat

On her my yearnings have no effect
Kindness from her I cannot expect

Into her street I go every day
To see her beauty, if only I may

Me her guards all love to mistreat
Her dogs me even would like to eat

Only her my heart and soul pursue
Her image is always in my view

If feelings in her I cannot stir
I would like to give my life for her

Of life she is the fountainhead
She can heal the sick and raise the dead

Given her, KHUSRO, you have renown
Now she has become the talk of the town

87 Aashiqaan ra dard e baimerham khush ast

The lovers seem to like the pain
They do not mind to cry in vain

They cannot talk about the girls
Without you telling about their curls

They also want their loves to know
Whatever hardships they undergo

They ask their darlings not to hurt
And not to treat them like some dirt

And when they see their flying hair
They tell themselves beware, beware!

Their beautiful faces they want to see
But if they cannot, they let it be

And KHUSRO also does not care
As long as his heart is caught in the hair

88 Muflisi az paadshaaie khushter ast

I would rather be poor than be a king
And piety, O preacher, is not my thing

So many woes the kings have to bear
The poor have nothing; they don't care

What's the use of having the wealth?
If you do not have your health

I do not want the arrogance and pride
Let me be humble and be dignified

The pangs of love it's better to endure
Than go and beg someone for a cure

I would rather be sinful, bad, and flawed
Than be a sheikh and be a fraud

The kings, O KHUSRO, don't you applaud
Just have in your heart the love of God

89 Aey, dahaanat chashma e aab e hayaat

Her mouth is the source of life's spring
The dead to life her kiss can bring

Oh, how I wish she'd come to me
And make my pain and sorrow flee

And how in her absence I cry and cry
Without her surely I'm going to die

With pain, and sorrow, and deep distress
Without her my life is meaningless

Whoever sees her beautiful face
Falls in love with her charm and grace

Though peace and quiet does KHUSRO prefer
He couldn't help falling in love with her

90 Aey, keh roo e to hayaat e jaan ast

Your charming eye is the source of life
Though every lash is like a knife

Your face does shine like the sun at noon
And gives the glow to the radiant moon

Your words, my dear, on your sugary lip
Like the drops of honey they collect and drip

Every lip but yours that I happen to kiss
Your sugar and honey in it I miss

Without you crying, I've lost my sight
My day is dark like the darkest night

And then you tell me, "Don't feel blue"
It's easy to say but hard to do

Beware of KHUSRO! He is breathing fire
Don't you come close; just let him expire

91 Aey dil, ghameen mabaash kah jaanaan raseedaniest

Rejoice, O heart, she is going to bring
With her, when she comes, the life's spring

The pain of parting you won't have to endure
For the ailment of yours she has the cure

Prepare your garden to revel and regale
For your rose is coming, O nightingale

Your love, O moth, you must proclaim
By burning yourself in her divine flame

With blood from heart her path you mark
When comes she strolling into the park

And when she comes, you thank your star
You don't know, KHUSRO, how lucky you are

92 Aey aarzoo e deeda, dilam dar hawa e tust

Oh, how I love you, the apple of my eye
My soul is your captive; you cannot deny

Whatever you say and whatever you do
It always increases my love for you

Treat it the way you want to treat
As always, my head is at your feet

To you I have given my soul, my life
Kill me if you like; here is the knife

My tearful eyes with blood I've fed
So now there's nothing left to be shed

For your juicy lips does KHUSRO crave
So give him a kiss; he is your slave

93 Aey baad, az aan bahaar khabar deh keh ta kujaast

Where is my gal, O breeze of spring?
From her a message did you bring?

Oh, was she going with another guy
Or was she alone when riding by?

My pain and sorrow are killing me
Did she ever ask you, "How is he"?

Without her, poison I sit and sip
Oh, how I miss her sugary lip

I wish someday with her sleepy eyes
She'll come to me to hypnotize

To KHUSRO a message you did bring
But where is she, O breeze of spring?

94 Aan Turk e naazneen keh jahaanay shikaar e oast

That Turko girl, she rules us all
We're the captives of that lovely doll

For her I'll give my life, my soul
Of my heart and mind she has control

I love her mouth, her cheeks, her eyes
Her face I adore and idolize

She is so splendid, so high, so proud
To touch her even I'm not allowed

She took my heart and gave me pain
But I'm so happy; I can't complain

Says KHUSRO, for her since you so much crave
If you can't be a friend, be her slave

95 Laal e labat ba chaashni az angbeen beh ast

Your lips are sweeter than the sweetest honey
And there is no bunny like you, my bunny

When saw the sky your glow and shine
It said, "This moon is better than mine"

The park has cypress and conifer and pine
But nothing like you, my cypress divine

You need no dagger, no sword, no knife
A dart from your eye can take my life

The fire of love is very, very nice
This hell is better than the paradise

Kiss your KHUSRO's eyes, you silly girl
His every little tear is like a pearl

96 Az aan gahay keh dil e mun ba soo e yaar e mun ast

Now that she has stolen my heart
Her love from me will never depart

Being a captive of her curly hair
My helpless heart, it hasn't a prayer

Me, O preacher, please don't hate
If I'm a toper, it's my fate

For when I drink, I'm like a king
Among the birds and flowers of spring

Time and again, I tell my heart
That love is pungent, bitter, and tart

Though lovers are not in a very good shape
The girls face annoyance that they can't escape

By now has KHUSRO had his fill
Him she should come and promptly kill

97 Zay bus keh goash e jahaanay pur az fughaan e mun ast

Everyone knows my sorrow and pain
My tale is heard in every domain

First she wounds it with her dart
Then she comes and bags my heart

O please for my life do not pray
For alive she doesn't want me to stay

And for my ailment there is no cure
The pain of parting I cannot endure

By love, like a moth, I'm badly stung
Like a burning candle, I've a fiery tongue

For her though, KHUSRO, I yearn and pine
I am also sure she'll never be mine

98 Zay khoon e dil keh ba rukhsaar maajra e mun ast

Though tears of blood do tell my tale
My crying for her I cannot curtail

Though feelings in her I cannot stir
I hope she knows I'm dying for her

From loving her I cannot abstain
She gives me though a lot of pain

O gardener, I know you'll concur
Nothing in the garden is like her

I know, O heart, you suffer the pain
But you're also a pain; you drive me insane

O KHUSRO, go and cry in her street
Maybe with you she'll come and meet

99   Rukhay wilaayat e chashm e puraab ra bagrift

Her lovely face and my tearful eye
Her curly hair and my grieving sigh

I cannot sleep when she isn't there
The pain of parting I cannot bear

Her mouth's the source of life's spring
The dead to life her kiss can bring

Her lips whenever I want to kiss
She looks at me and just says – hiss!

When sees the moon her shine and grace
Behind the clouds it hides its face

When KHUSRO wants to play with her hair
She grins and says, "Don't you dare!"

100   Cheh daaghhaast keh ber seena e figaaram neest

Is there a wish that's not in my heart?
And is there a pain that's not in her dart?

I tried and tried but didn't succeed
My pleas and prayers she'll never heed

In love I've nothing but pain and shame
And no one is there who I can blame

I tried to hide but it was a bust
My tearful eyes I cannot trust

I pray to God that when I die
She'll come to me and just say hi

And when I'm dying, she'll say, "Gee whiz
What a hapless lover my KHUSRO is"

101 Sapeeda dam keh zamaana zay rukh naqaab andaakht

In the depth of darkness, with the hope all gone
Through the veil of night came the light of dawn

The golden light, while I was asleep
Broke the charming spell of my slumber deep

The hosts of the stars, it having overrun
Wearing the golden crown came the morning sun

In the sea of night, with a deadly harpoon
The mighty sun had bagged the moon

And the sun, its conquest, to glorify
Had spilled the blood all over the sky

Like him, to KHUSRO, there is no one
For the king is so like the mighty sun

102 Her shab dilam zay dast e khayaalat zaboon shawad

When I think of her I get an ache
I feel as if my heart will break

When she looks at me, I feel a dart
Going through and through my woeful heart

And when, like moon, she shines at night
She expels the gloom from me outright

And when in the park she takes a stroll
Instantly on my heart I lose control

And if she does ever about me inquire
With love my heart she sets on fire

But when she, KHUSRO, flirts with my foe
I get very angry; I feel very low

103 Kujaast dil keh ghamat ra nihaan tawaanad daasht

Is there a lover who can hide the pain
And bear it quietly and not complain?

Sitting with the rival, she tries to pry
On me, though ignoring, she keeps an eye

And when my rival is fighting with me
She stays as neutral as she can be

And though I've many, there is no friend
On whose discretion I can really depend

But she is so gorgeous, so graceful, so grand
That when compared, the moon looks bland

Though someone as lovely is difficult to find
I only wish, KHUSRO, that she were more kind

104 Nigaar e mun keh ba junbeedan e saba khuftast

Without you, O breeze, she cannot sleep
So track of her you must surely keep

Going to her, you should lightly tread
Especially if she is already in bed

When she is sleeping, her beautiful eyes
They still enchant and mesmerize

And while she sleeps, her lovers weep
Even in their graves they cannot sleep

And even the folks who think they're wise
The effect of her magic they cannot disguise

So, KHUSRO, with joy I'll surely scream
Even if she comes only in my dream

105 Raseed fasl e gul o baad unberafshaanast

The flowers are blooming with scent in the air
And the girls are also very lovely and fair

The birds are flying with great fanfare
With the conifers swinging in the park everywhere

The iris is happy and full of spunk
With the dew in the cup, the tulip is drunk

Like in the ears of the beautiful girls
The drops of dew look like the pearls

In short, the garden with the flowers of spring
Looks like the court of our noble king

May the flowers of the king be never stale
May he always keep KHUSRO as a nightingale

106 Her keh der paish e chashm e roshan e maast

The beautiful girl that brightens my eyes
Oh, how my heart she does terrorize

The glow and glamour of her gorgeous face
Makes the glory of the moon look commonplace

My tears of blood, though such a disgrace
Do give some color to my colorless face

My faith and creed, it has made me sell
This love in my heart of an infidel

Though, KHUSRO, love can cause blight
Its fire can also be a source of light

107   Turk e mastam keh qasd e eimaan daasht

I've lost not only my faith, my creed
For the gals I could lose my life indeed

My blood they want instead of the wine
On my roasted heart they like to dine

When they see me cry, those beautiful girls
They think my tears are so like pearls

But the spring is here and the air is nice
It has come, it seems, from the paradise

The air, when the flowers it does beguile
They blush, they glow, they beam, they smile

And when it touches my loving soul
The poor little heart, it loses control

But I can't win, KHUSRO, I'm going to lose
Between love and life I'll simply have to choose

108   Her keh roo e to deed jaan daanist

Everybody loves her lovely face
For it has beauty, charm, and grace

Her lips are juicy, luscious, and red
Her kiss can revive even the dead

And the darling dimple of her dainty chin
If you don't kiss it, it would be a sin

So when she leaves me, I cry and cry
I don't want to live; I would rather die

I feel sometimes my death is close
And I'm only fit for the vultures and crows

My love has made me so frail and weak
I can barely move; I can hardly speak

But there was a time, as KHUSRO knows
I had no worries; I had no woes

109 Sar e zulf e to ta bajunbeedast

Her golden curls when they fly in the air
Their fragrance goes in the world everywhere

And when you smell the musk somewhere
You can be sure that my gal is there

But the smell of blood is also there
Whenever a heart does bleed somewhere

And when you see a heart on fire
In it there's always a burning desire

And when my love is out of my sight
It all goes dark; there is no light

And when she tells me she's going to leave
Stop her I cannot; I can only grieve

This whole thing, KHUSRO, is so unfair
I love her so much but she doesn't care

110 Nigaar e mun imshab sar e naaz daasht

She is so beautiful, so elegant, so proud
But to talk of my love I'm not allowed

My feelings for her that are deep inside
The moment I see her, I just can't hide

Resist her I cannot, she looks so divine
Whenever she takes a little bit of wine

Tangled I get in the golden curls
For a weakness I have for the beautiful girls

And a slave I am of the charming eyes
With a look they enchant, they mesmerize

And their every glance is like a dart
It jabs, it stabs, it wounds my heart

And being in love I can only wail
For, KHUSRO, I am a nightingale

111 Gulistaan naseem e saher yaaftast

Blowing in the garden is the morning breeze
And the flowers are flirting with the birds and the bees

The primrose is proud and looks so grand
Has a tulip in waiting with a cup in hand

The birds are feeling very hearty and hale
And singing a song is the nightingale

In a place like this though I should be glad
But she is not here and I'm so sad

This waiting and watching although I hate
I have no choice but to watch and wait

So, KHUSRO, I sit and wait all night
Hoping I'll see her before sunlight

112 Butay kaz wayam roo ba deewaangiest

I love her so much, I must be mad
So if she kills me it won't be so bad

With a look she can always take my life
She needs no dagger, no sword, no knife

Whenever I try to play with her hair
She tells me sternly, "Oh, don't you dare!"

And the closer to her that I try to be
The farther away she sits from me

But wherever I go, she stays in my mind
Her mental image I can't leave behind

And, KHUSRO, her beauty spot is my bait
To become her prey I just can't wait

113 Ger tura naaz o badkhooie een ast

My gal is full of vanity and pride
And a stony heart she has inside

And although she doesn't care for my heart
From it her love will never, never part

This love has set my heart on fire
Her kind attention it will now require

I hope to God that before I die
She'll come at least to say good-bye

For when she leaves me, I cry and cry
I moan, I groan, I sob, I sigh

But expect I cannot any favor from her
For I'm not, KHUSRO, her only lover

114 Bahaar aamad o gulha e bostaan bashaguft

The flowers are blooming and the spring is here
Let's go with our friends and drink some beer

Singing to the rose is the nightingale
The topers are swinging and drinking the ale

The birds, like lovers, kissing the cheeks
Are smooching the roses with eager beaks

And drinking are the beautiful girls red wine
As if it is blood from the heart of mine

With tulips and roses in the crimson attire
It looks like the park has been set on fire

And about his gal as KHUSRO talks
Converge do the people to him in flocks

115 Yaar chun baa mast behr e deedanash taajeel cheest

What's in my heart, I don't have to see
And closer than that she just can't be

With the flames and fire and all the rest
A temple of love I have made my breast

With her, my predator, so ready to slay
I just can't wait to become her prey

A mystic has hurdles he cannot evade
But being a lover he can't be dismayed

So pain and sorrow he must endure
For the pangs of love there is no cure

And a pious man a lover can't be
For he cannot practice hypocrisy

So give not to KHUSRO any advice
For love, O preacher, he'll pay any price

116 Az mun aan kaamyaab ra cheh gham ast

My pain and sorrow if I cannot bear
How dark is the night, the moon doesn't care

Whatever may happen to a speck of dirt
The glowing sun it just can't hurt

And if her lover can't sleep at night
What does it matter, she sleeps alright

How many moths does burn a flame?
What does it care, it is only a game

If innocent people he has to kill
To a soldier it's only a part of the drill

And a fish, O KHUSRO, whether it lives or dies
The ocean can't bother to scrutinize

117 Ya Rab, cheh shud kaan
Turk e ma tark e mohibbaan karda ast

Oh, why for her lovers she does not care?
And why does she lead them to such despair?

Oh, do not tell her about their pain
She won't be sorry; there's nothing to gain

But there was a time when she was kind
And being with her lovers she didn't mind

But now her lovers do cry and cry
They moan, they groan, they sob, they sigh

And if they smell the scent of her hair
They simply go crazy; their clothes they tear

And be not surprised when you discover
That like them KHUSRO is also a lover

118 Khayaal e roo e to chu durr e naab dar nazar ast

I am in love with her ruby lips
From them every word like honey drips

She is tall and slim like a cypress tree
And when she walks, it's something to see

And her curly hair, when it flies in the air
You can smell it's fragrance in the world everywhere

And you should also see her dreamy eyes
They charm, they enchant, they mesmerize

Her curls are as dark as the darkest night
And the shine of her face is like moonlight

And you should see KHUSRO how he flips
Whenever he sees her mouth and lips

119 Ba khud mabeen keh chu roo e to aaftaabay hast

Your face is like the sun at noon
And to its beauty no one is immune

Its glorious glow you cannot curtail
It cannot be hidden behind the veil

Your every glance is like a dart
It jabs, it stabs, it wounds the heart

A fire in the breast it can also start
And burn and fry and roast the heart

Your mouth is like a budding rose
And everybody loves your precious nose

But when there are tears in your charming eyes
Not only KHUSRO, but the whole world cries

120 Rukhash badeedam o guftam keh bostaan een ast

Her face is like a beautiful rose
With a smile she can cure a lover's woes

Listening to her is quite a treat
Even when bitter, she sounds so sweet

Her braided hair is like a rope
With which if bound, one has no hope

Her love has made me weak and frail
I've lost my pep; I look so pale

And when I say that she should be kind
She thinks that I am out of my mind

But generous, KHUSRO, she can also be
And bestow a lot of favors on me

121 Zay mun dar hijr e o her dam fughaan e zaar meeaayad

The ones unlucky, they sigh and cry
For the favored one the limit is sky

I so much want to sit by her gate
But the keeper of the gate I can't placate

Oh, how in her absence I cry and cry
Without my darling I'll surely die

The whole world listens whenever she talks
And everybody loves the way she walks

Of lovers, O mystic, it is a club
The secrets of love you find in the pub

And KHUSRO's in love with a lovely maid
Of the pangs of love he is not afraid

122 Saba meejunbad o aan mast e ma ra khaab meeaayad

All night she sleeps while I cry and cry
I moan, I groan, I sob, I sigh

She is my moon; without her light
I have no use for the moonlit night

When burns my heart in the dark of night
I envy all those who sleep so tight

But once in a while when I see her cry
I feel as if I'm going to die

I tell her on him she cannot rely
Because my rival is an awful guy

Then, KHUSRO, armed with every frill
This faithful lover she comes to kill

123   Zamistaan meerawad ayyaam e gulha paish meeaayad

With flowers in hand when she comes to me
I'm so surprised; I can only say gee!

And when her curls do fly in the air
The sight my heart just cannot bear

And when she goes strolling in the park
In the flowers she kindles of envy the spark

And when he sees her lips so red
Even the wisest man does lose his head

And when of love she lights the fire
In the heart he feels a burning desire

And when with a glance, she throws a dart
It stabs, it jabs, it wounds his heart

And, KHUSRO, he loves her long eyelashes
For they fill his heart with a million slashes

124   Mara baaz az tareeq e saaqi e khud yaad meeaayad

My girl in the bar, oh, how I miss
Because with her I find the bliss

Without this gal I'm totally stuck
But when she is back, I'm back in luck

Away from her I can never stay
Though she's a predator, and I'm a prey

The thrill in my heart I cannot bear
Whenever I remember her curly hair

And soon of it I do become aware
That the scent of her hair is there everywhere

But, KHUSRO, you shouldn't listen to me
I'm like all lovers, so let me be

125 Cheh shud kaan sarv e seemandaam soo e mun nameeaayad

Oh, why my love doesn't come to me?
And why from me does she always flee?

My blood you tell her not to spill
For then there will be no one to kill

If wounds and scars she would like to see
She should look in my heart, for there they'll be

And tell her, when she is out of my sight
My vision is dark; there is no light

Of light in my eyes remains no trace
If see they cannot her glorious face

And tell her, KHUSRO, to use a chain
For a lover like me who is so insane

126 Ba gulgasht e chaman chun gulsitaan e mun baroon aayad

Strolling whenever she comes to the park
Of love in the heart she lights a spark

When I think of her I begin to cry
And I feel as if I'm going to die

On the Day of Judgment when people meet
They will find me buried in her street

And when they'll ask, I was killed by whom?
I'll have to tell them, she brought my doom

And if they inquire I'll further say
I died when she left me and went away

If, KHUSRO, in the end push came to shove
I'll have to confess that I died of love

127 Maroo zeensaan keh her soo jaama e jaan chaak khahad shud

The way she walks, it tears my heart
And with a look from her it falls apart

And if I'm burnt, she is not to blame
For I'm the moth, and she is the flame

Her every glance is like a dart
So it's not her fault if it wounds my heart

And when she hurts me, I do not complain
For when she's sorry, I feel the pain

So, KHUSRO, my gal you should go and meet
For even when tart, she's very, very sweet

128 Seemeen zanakh keh turra e unberfishaan burd

Her ruby lips with a charming grin
Her fragrant hair and the dimpled chin

She's tall, and poised, and slim, and trim
When sees her cypress, it becomes so grim

Though love has pang, and pain, and sting
This pain of parting is a terrible thing

And our reason though is a useful guide
No guidance in love can it ever provide

So when I think of her I cry and cry
And I feel as if I am going to die

For her my life I'm willing to give
Without her, KHUSRO, I just can't live

129   Hunoozat naaz gird e chashm e khaabaalood meegerdad

Those beautiful dreamy, charming eyes
Oh, how they enchant and mesmerize

Her every glance is a deadly dart
Oh, how it wounds my woeful heart

With the pain of parting, oh, how I smart
Even though she's always there in my heart

The fire of love, when it burns my heart
Even she does feel it, though far apart

And, KHUSRO, with pain whenever I cry
With sighs I shake the earth and the sky

130   Hama shab der dilam aan kafir e khoonkhaar meegerdad

I miss her so when I see moonlight
I toss and turn in the bed all night

She needs no dagger, no sword, no knife
With a single glance she can take my life

So lovely, so dainty, so charming, so fair
Like her a flower there isn't anywhere

And when in her absence I cry and sigh
People feel so sorry, they also cry

But, KHUSRO, whenever I go to her street
Me her dogs even don't want to meet

131 Een dil keh her shabaysh zay saalay fazoon rawad

This love has become a constant grind
Oh, how I've lost my peace of mind

On me it has surely taken its toll
My love is totally out of control

All night I shed in tears my blood
And often this flow becomes a flood

She breaks my heart and does not care
And then she insists on staying in there

And when she leaves, she leaves no trace
Though I yearn and yearn to see her face

This misery of love I cannot escape
So, KHUSRO, I am in a very bad shape

132 Ager aan jaadoo e khoonkhaara
nargis dar fasoon aarad

When she looks at me, her dreamy eyes
My peace and sleep they compromise

I wish she'll come and take control
And bring some peace to my woeful soul

O breeze, next time when you go to her street
Do bring for my eyes the dirt of her feet

Oh, how I worship her curly hair
Its twist, and turn, its trap, and snare

When they look at me, they think it's sad
But I am so happy that I am mad

And, KHUSRO, I have no hopes, no fears
All night I shed my blood in tears

133 Mia ghamzazanaan bairoon keh hooay dar jahaan uftad

When she comes walking down the street
Watching her steps is quite a treat

And though she would think it's indiscreet
I would like to fall and die at her feet

And when my carcass in the dump she throws
I'd like to be eaten by the vultures and crows

I hope with my rivals she won't get drunk
For that would leave me in a lot of funk

And though I think it is not very fair
For me, I know, she does not care

But, KHUSRO, a lover cannot complain
He cannot be bothered by loss or gain

134 Chun zulfash fitna shud bar jaan, dilam aabaad kay maanad

My heart goes wild when I think of your hair
And away from you I have great despair

O please don't scold me if I complain
I cannot be quiet when I'm in pain

The glow of your face makes me totally blind
When I see your eyes, I lose my mind

And don't you blame me for loving you
A beauty like you everyone wants to woo

Longing for Juliet no Romeo can cease
And away from her he can't be at peace

So loving you, darling, I cannot shun
For KHUSRO says, lovers can't reason

135   Cheh poashi perda ber rooay keh aan pinhaan nameemaanad

Your face from your lovers O please don't hide
They have come to see you from far and wide

Being a lowly tramp, I don't have appeal
But my love for you I cannot conceal

You have the elegance, and charm, and grace
And everyone adores your beautiful face

A man who sees your enchanting eyes
The allure for you he cannot disguise

For me, I admit, you do not care
That things can change, I am also aware

Be nice to your KHUSRO, and never say never
For charity and goodness do live forever

136   Chun jaan e aashiqaan aan maah ra sultaan o khaan saazad

She is my queen and I'm her slave
About her always I rave and rave

Strolling whenever she goes to the park
Wherever she goes she makes her mark

And everyone loves her magical eyes
They charm, they enchant, they mesmerize

And her, for burning, I cannot blame
For I'm the moth, and she's the flame

My pain and sorrow it does not decrease
Though I go to her street to find my peace

But, KHUSRO, this love, though it's an abyss
I find in your verses the eternal bliss

137 Hama masti e khalq az saaghar o paimaana meekhaizad

The tavern though I do patronize
I only get drunk when I see her eyes

Oh, I'm so happy and feel so blessed
That the fire of love is burning in my breast

When I tell the people my woeful tale
It touches their hearts; they begin to wail

And when in her street I go and cry
Even the watchmen there starts to sigh

And if I'm burnt, she is not to blame
For I 'm the moth, and she is the flame

And though to many it's only a dot
It drives me crazy, her beauty spot

There's so much, O KHUSRO, that I can do
But a shrew like her I cannot subdue

138 Hawaay meerasad kaz sar gareebaan chaak khaham zad

This love is driving me insane
My craving for her I cannot contain

Oh, how, in her absence, I cry and cry
Without her surely I'm going to die

My tears of blood are making me blind
But what can I do, she's so unkind?

Her love has set my heart on fire
It's going to burn my being entire

And no matter how much I try to be smart
O KHUSRO, I can never soften her heart

69

139 Cheh khush subhey dameed imshab mara az roo e yaar e khud

In the depth of darkness with the hope all gone
She finally came as the light of dawn

After seeing me all night in great agony
My lady luck took pity on me

Seeing her face was so very nice
I thought I was truly in paradise

O please don't ask me about my pain
For me it's something difficult to explain

Know I do not where to start
I feel so sorry for my poor little heart

And though she thinks it's so indiscreet
Whenever I see her, I kiss her feet

Me her worship does not demean
For I am a beggar, and she's my queen

And though her, KHUSRO, I'd like to embrace
I'm lucky if only I can see her face

140 Daroagh o raasti kan ghamza e ghammaaz paiwandad

Oh, how she plays with your poor little heart
She can put it together and take it apart

Her every glance is a deadly dart
It can jab, and stab, and wound your heart

She will sometimes come and be with you
And then she'll see you and not say boo

Your heart for her is only a toy
She'll play with it and then destroy

So when with you she tries to flirt
You ought to be careful and remain alert

And don't you, KHUSRO, become her prey
Away from her you should try to stay

141   Butay koo her damam
dishnaamha e shakkareen bakhshad

Though when she scolds me, it's not very funny
But even when bitter, she is sweet like honey

And I like it not a bit when she
Commends my rival in front of me

But when she flirts and gives me a smile
To me my sorrow becomes worthwhile

And she is so sweet that I can condone
Even when she hits my face with a stone

To my faith and reason I say farewell
When I see my beautiful infidel

And, KHUSRO, I've loved her for years and years
And all this time I have only shed tears

142   Shum e mun ager yak shab az khaana beroon aayad

At night when she comes with her glowing face
She draws the moths from all over the place

Her lovers all she knocks out flat
By the way she wears her beautiful hat

Whenever she hears a madman's groans
Like kids she throws at him the stones

And my rival whenever she goes to see
She acts as if she does not know me

And burning me to death is always her aim
For I am the moth, and she is the flame

For my gal, O KHUSRO, it is no sweat
She can kill her lover without regret

143 Aan dil ba cheh kaar aayad kaan khaana e to nabwad

Oh, take my wounded heart in your care
And tie it up with your braided hair

Your faithful servant I humbly remain
Your love has made me totally insane

Me peace of mind only you can give
Without you, darling, I just can't live

Your curls on your face I do love a lot
And I'm so crazy about your beauty spot

My soul is burning with love and desire
Only you, my love, can put out this fire

And KHUSRO will tell you how I cry and cry
And how, in your absence, I'm going to die

144 Darda keh digger ma ra aan yaar nameepursad

For me my beloved cares not a bit
This business of love I would like to quit

By always asking and looking for her
A whole lot of trouble I often incur

But there was a time when she was kind
Someone more caring you could not find

Oh, how much pain do I have to endure?
When all my ailments she can instantly cure

Yes her, O KHUSRO, I know I demean
For I'm a beggar, and she's the queen

145 Ta ghamza e khoonraiz e to qasd e dil e ma kard

When she trains on my heart her deadly glance
It has no recourse; it doesn't have a chance

To her if someone tries to be close
He loses forever his peace and repose

Oh, why can't she be a little less unkind?
And why to my yearning she's totally blind?

A little more loving oh, why can't she be?
And why keeps she always away from me?

But there was a time when she was very nice
For not being thankful I'm now paying the price

So I had a chance and it I blew
Now I don't know, KHUSRO, what I can do?

146 Yak dil ba sar e koo e to aabaad nayaaband

Everyone is a captive of your curly hair
And those, who love you, are all in despair

Wherever they look, it's a total mess
Your lovers are all in great distress

And when you go out after drinking wine
Even the preachers think that you are divine

For your lovers you've no time to spare
What happens to them, you simply don't care

For you unto death your lovers crave
And carry to the graves the wounds you gave

And having lost his heart, he can't even cry
So one day your KHUSRO will quietly die

147   Sad jaan ba yakay daang ba bazaar faroashand

These beautiful shoppers are so very smart
With just one look they can buy your heart

Instead of the goods to keep in the cellars
They go to the market and buy up the sellers

But no matter how much they're willing to spend
I'll never, never give up my beautiful friend

With it though I am very willing to part
There's no one there who wants my heart

So don't you go after a beautiful gal
For it's not good for a lover's morale

And you know, KHUSRO, she's like a hawk
She's not going to fall for your sweet little talk

148   Hindoo e mara kushtan e turkaana babeeneed

Since I'm in love with my infidel
A million idols in my little heart dwell

Oh, how I love her dreamy eyes
They charm, they enchant, they mesmerize

Her flaming cheeks inflame the desire
For I'm the moth; I love the fire

I'm only a tramp, so poor, so mean
And she's my kind and generous queen

And KHUSRO, when he talks about her lips
His verses in milk and honey he dips

149 Booay zay sar e zulf e nigaareen ba mun aareed

Bring, O breeze, the scent of her hair
Without her I am in great despair

Oh, take me to the bar and make me drunk
For I have no hope, and I'm in a funk

An offer of wine I cannot decline
And even in my grave I'll miss my wine

With pain and sorrow I'm falling apart
Oh, what do I do with my woeful heart?

My pain and suffering I cannot explain
Without her, KHUSRO, I'm going insane

150 Baad aamad o zaan sarv e kharamaan khaber aawurd

Go bring some news of my gal, O breeze
And put my heart and soul at ease

It makes me merrily drunk, I swear
When it brings me her scent, this morning air

But when the fire in my heart reappears
To put it out I use my tears

My flower when sees a nightingale
It falls in love and starts to wail

And when she takes too long to write
I'm not very happy; I become uptight

I simply then, KHUSRO, go to her street
And rub my eyes on the dirt of her feet

151 Yak khanda bazan zaan lab e laal e shakeraalood

On your ruby lips do put on a smile
To make the pangs of your love worthwhile

Your lover is wounded; he's weak and frail
Do let him tell you his sorrowful tale

His wounded heart does bleed and bleed
You can see his blood in your street indeed

For your sugary lips he yearns like a bee
He's stuck on them; he can never flee

Your pain of parting he feels so deep
That he would not eat; that he would not sleep

But KHUSRO says, in the dirt of your feet
He finds the cure of his ills complete

152 Aey zulf e to daam e dil e daana o khiradmand

Your curls can trap the wisest of men
But how they can do it, is beyond my ken

And after they fall in love with you
Oh, how to their wisdom they say adieu

And even when you tell them a lie
It sounds so sweet, they instantly buy

And when your curls do fly in the air
Their love and passion they simply can't bear

That people in love so heave and grieve
The men who lust can't ever believe

That lovers their love who cannot hide
They think they're so very undignified

And love, they say, is like a bog
And KHUSRO is nothing but a branded dog

153 Aaqil nadahad aashiq e dilsokhta ra pand

To a lover, O wise man, you don't give advice
And punish him you do not; you try to be nice

Oh, he is like Jacob mourning his son
So have some pity, and don't make fun

In the land of love your wisdom you shun
For a mad man there is the real wise one

There yearning and longing are a lover's lot
The fire in his heart you just can't blot

He is born to suffer; so it's no surprise
That he loves and loves until he dies

And KHUSRO is helpless; he's also a lover
And the bondage on freedom he's born to prefer

154 Tarsam keh az atraaf e jahaan dood baraayad

The sigh of a lover has so much fire
It can fill with smoke the world entire

The scent of his girl when smells a lover
His heart does emit the fragrance of myrrh

It so does ignite in his heart the fire
That hide he cannot his burning desire

And even if his darling does ask for his life
He does not demur; he offers her a knife

His Juliet's beauty he loves so much
That him even Romeo in it can't touch

And for her elegance he does so crave
That song of his love he sings in his grave

But is spite of it all, if he wants to succeed
A lot of luck, KHUSRO, he surely does need

155   Sarvay chu to dar khalkh wa naushaad nabaashad

O without your cypress no garden is gay
Those palms and pines look all so gray

Oh, how you break the heart of your lover
And how you enjoy his utter dismay

You also like to disgrace the fellow
And want him to like it, and say hurray

His utter dependence you seem to relish
And you want him so much to stay that way

But since it makes you so very upset
His pain and sorrow he cannot display

And because you happen to be so callous
Your stony heart he never can sway

But your KHUSRO also loves so much your eyes
That without them his verse he cannot say

156   Yek roaz ba umray zay munat yaad niayad

Anyone who enters your neighborhood
He'll never be happy, it's understood

The breeze from your street, when it does depart
It comes and stokes the fire in my heart

And even after death for you it'll crave
I wish you'll come to visit my grave

In the twists and turns of your curly hair
My heart is caught in a deadly snare

And even in spring when the birds are gay
It yearns and yearns to become your prey

And it goes like crazy from place to place
To catch a glimpse of your enchanting face

And KHUSRO says, it's no surprise
That it can shake the world whenever it cries

157 Roozay agar aan maah ba mehmaan e mun aayad

If she'd only choose to be with me
I'll become the lord of the land and sea

My heart is crazy; it is gone for good
Would it ever be back? No likelihood!

When the breeze does bring the scent of her hair
The pain of her absence my heart can't bear

But although it does bitterly complain
It thoroughly enjoys the pang and pain

It also thinks it would be a treat
If in the end it could die at her feet

And it also says she won't be so severe
If it's moaning, KHUSRO, she could only hear

158 Dil basta e baala e yakay tangqaba shud

My heart went after a tight skirt
It thought it'll flirt, but just got hurt

The others are happy because they're sane
But it's so crazy, it enjoys the pain

And my passion does make my heart despair
It's lost all patience; it cannot forbear

And whenever she sees it falling apart
She loves to come and trample my heart

But when on a horse she passes me by
It cannot resist her; it likes to fly

And KHUSRO its passion it cannot curtail
So like dust it follows and forms her trail

159 Aabaad na shud dil keh kharaab e pisaraan shud

Whenever they see it, look how they bubble
These lovers of beauty, they're always in trouble

But all her beauty would've gone to waste
If there were no lovers who had the taste

So the rubies with which herself she covers
Are nothing but the bleeding hearts of her lovers

Look how a man who thinks he's smart
Behaves like a fool when he follows his heart

Oh, how he yearns, and cries, and cries
And how many time for a beauty he dies

And KHUSRO is also a lover of beauty
And a beauty he loves as a matter of duty

160 Dil neest keh dar way gham e dildaar nagunjad

You cannot love without feeling blue
But without it also you cannot do

And love with reason you cannot mix
For a bleeding heart you just can't fix

And when in love, don't ever complain
For you can't have love without the pain

And a beautiful girl, no matter how nice
You cannot get without paying the price

And her ruby lips you cannot touch
Without the cost that's simply too much

And the rules of love you cannot flout
And, KHUSRO, once in, you can't get out

161 Yaaram chun ba khanda shaker e basta kushaayad

Whenever she gives her lovers a smile
Their sorrow and pain become worthwhile

And when she looks with her dreamy eyes
Their restless hearts she does hypnotize

And when she tightens the belt on her waist
They love her style; they adore her taste

And the birds and the flowers begin to sigh
From the park when she leaves like a butterfly

And when at home, she shuts her door
Oh, how her lovers she does ignore

And when to them she wouldn't say hi
Her lovers, O KHUSRO, oh, how they cry

162 Jaay guzarat, aey but e chaalaak, nayuftad

Oh, when she would not look at me
I become as wretched as I can be

And out at night when she wouldn't go
The moon and the stars lose all their glow

Her lover's blood she loves to shed
And sheds it until the place is red

When she wants to kill me, I wholly concur
For I'm more than willing to die for her

And abuse at me she hurls and hurls
And thinks my tears are gems and pearls

And though of my sorrow she's completely aware
What happens to me, KHUSRO, she doesn't really care

163 Baraft aan dil keh ba sabr aashna bood

The heart that loved and could forbear
It has finally left for God knows where

Now night after night I cannot sleep
For I find her fragrance always in the air

And I wail and wail like a nightingale
Because her absence I just can't bear

But being a lover, I should realize
That the beautiful girls are always unfair

And that when he sees her lovely face
Even our preacher doesn't have a prayer

And if he dares to knock at her door
For him, he is told, she does not care

And when she sees him, she pulls her sword
For the killing of her KHUSRO she thinks is fair

164 Shakar paish e labat sheereen nagooyand

Her lips with honey you cannot compare
To call her a flower would be unfair

And although she has a stony heart
To call it that would not be smart

And a heart, when you see, caught in her hair
Don't call her curl a trap or a snare

And a man who worships a beautiful doll
Him an idolater you should not call

And if there's a lover who cannot forbear
Scorn him not; he needs your prayer

And in KHUSRO you'll find a cavalier
Even Romeo to him comes nowhere near

165 Ba her dard o ghamay dil mubtila shud

Oh, how my heart does ache and ache
And how her lover she does forsake

And how it hurts, she does not know
That being my love, she loves my foe

So when they see me cry and cry
My neighbors think I'm going to die

I used to think that the lovers are mad
But now I'm sorry, and I feel so sad

Oh, when my darling steals a heart
She looks so pious; she feels so smart

And though to all she's nice and kind
To the woes of her KHUSRO she's totally blind

166 Dilam zeensaan keh zaar o mubtila shud

The one for whom I'm so lovesick
She is cruel, and callous and a heartless chick

O what she wants, may she always get
And may she never have to regret

And all those faithful, that infidel
May she always have them under the spell

And in her garden, the nightingale
May he always cry, and moan, and wail

In the fire of love may he always burn
And may he yearn, and yearn, and yearn

And may her KHUSRO have the verve
To stay in love and to keep his nerve

167 Dil e aashiq chira shaida nabaashad

Without her love there can't be a heart
Though falling in love is not very smart

A lover of hers has nothing but despair
But she's very happy; she doesn't have a care

For like a flower she is full of glee
And has all the grace of a cypress tree

She's also as elegant as anyone can be
And her beauty even the blind can see

There can be no heart without her love
And yearning for her no head is above

And since he has seen her, KHUSRO swears
That for no one else in the world he cares

168 Dil e ma ra shakeeb az jaan nabaashad

You'll lose your patience; you'll lose your peace
Your pain and pang, O they'll never cease

And love with patience you cannot combine
You'll yearn, and yearn, and pine, and pine

The pangs of love you'll have to endure
You can cry and cry, but there is no cure

But love is also a great treasure
And the pain is not without the pleasure

And since your gal is a beautiful thing
Think of all the beauty your love does bring

169 Chaman ra rang o boo chandeen nabaashad

For the smell of flowers I do not care
If I cannot smell your fragrant hair

And all these rubies I would not miss
If your ruby lip I could only kiss

But you do not even bother to know
What's my sorrow, my grief, my woe

And because I worship a beautiful belle
Everyone thinks I am an infidel

But true it is, I must concede
That idol-worship is my only creed

So here I am, a troubled man
Who hurts himself whenever he can

170 Dil e mun khoon shud o jaanaan nadaanad

My heart, it bleeds but knows she not
And when I tell her, she just says - what?

O she can raise you from dead again
But she would never cure your pain

And it never listens; it's always sad
My wayward heart, it's totally mad

And they also say I'll go to hell
For the faithful think I'm an infidel

And the gal I love has a stony heart
And knows she not how it hurts to part

But I, her KHUSRO, am a nightingale
And without my rose I wail and wail

171 Khatay az laal e jaanaan meebaraayad

Her sweet and juicy red, red lips
Oh, how from them the honey drips

And her soft and curly raven hair
Oh, how they cover her face so fair

And her lovely face, so fair, so white
Like moon it brightens her lovers' night

But she's an idol who can mislead
And threaten the Faithfull's troth and creed

So, slave of her is KHUSRO's heart
It's locked in her locks, and cannot part

172 Sar e zulf e to yaari ra nashaayad

Friendly yes, but friend of none
Though loved by all, she loves no one

With the magic black, her charming eyes
They lure, they enchant, they mesmerize

And with just a look she can crucify
And make her lovers all cry and cry

And with her terrible anger out of control
She can wound your heart and bruise your soul

But her lovely smile can also mislead
And rob you of your faith and creed

And when KHUSRO goes and knocks at her door
Oh, how his prayers she does ignore

173   Az yaad e to dil juda na khahad shud

My darling, you I cannot forget
And falling in love I'll never regret

The bonds of love are hard to break
So my passion for you I cannot forsake

For love is an arrow, a deadly dart
It hits and does not leave the heart

And what a mess of the heart this arrow makes
For it bleeds, and bleeds, and aches, and aches

So now you know why KHUSRO craves
And why he's one of your many slaves

174   Naala bar aayad her taraf
kaan but kharaamaan dar rasad

O when in the garden she takes a walk
The birds shun flowers, and to her they flock

O soul of mine, don't be so glum
She might relent, and might yet come

My crazy heart, O please don't cry
I'm sure one day she will come by

But when she comes, she'll not stay
And that will add to your dismay

And if you died when she went away
It was your fate, she would simply say

So, as KHUSRO says, you shouldn't complain
For you can't have love without the pain

175 Ma ra cheh jaan baashad keh to bar ma fishaani naaz e khud

O please, my love, don't play with me
I take my romance very seriously

You flirt with them; they play with you
But it is a thing that I cannot do

For you, my love, I'm willing to die
So when you hurt me, I cry and cry

And even though you would like to know
To you my wounds I just can't show

And KHUSRO knows I would rather die
Than leave you, darling, and say good-bye

176 Meekhahad aan sarv e rawaan kamrooz dar sahra shawad

Even to the desert when my cypress goes
The birds all follow, in there to repose

The creatures there become all eyes
For her they adore and idolize

She makes her place in everyone's heart
And once in there, she does not depart

And carrying wine when she goes to the shrine
The mystics all there think she is divine

And KHUSRO being a nightingale
Her praise he sings in every little vale

177   Chand zay dour beenamat, weh
keh dilam kabab shud

My heart keeps bleeding since she has gone
And my nights are endless without her dawn

I cannot forget when we'd sit and drink
And all night long she'd smile and wink

She'd look like moon in a moonlit night
And the sun would borrow from her its light

And when her curls would cover her face
Like clouds they'd give her moon such grace

But when I'd declare my love for her
Her boundless wrath I would only incur

Then, KHUSRO, I'd sit and cry and cry
And they'd all feel sorry, even the passersby

178   Doash ma boodaem o aan mehroo,
shab e mehtaab bood

There was a time when things were right
And in moonlight we'd drink all night

And whatever I did wouldn't raise her brow
And all my advances she'd gladly allow

To me she was always very, very sweet
And for it I'd cry and kiss her feet

And turning pale, with my eyes red
Her deserting me I would greatly dread

And if I could not kiss her lip
I used to think, I'd simply flip

But, KHUSRO, now it is all a dream
And like a maniac, I scream and scream

179 Aey, khush aan waqtay keh aan badahd baa ma yaar bood

There was a time when she was so sweet
And I virtually used to live in her street

And I'd go to the park, holding her hand
To see the flowers and to hear the band

And when the birds would wing and sing
We would go in a trance, and dance, and swing

And then we would take a little bit of wine
And she'd sit by me and I would recline

But all this now has come to an end
She's totally forgotten that I was her friend

So it's no wonder; it's no surprise
That for so long I haven't closed my eyes

And KHUSRO says, it's now too late
There's nothing to be done; it's my fate

180 Ta jahaan bood az jahaan hargiz dilam khurram nabood

The world is full of sorrow and pain
And the hearts that love have to be insane

Our circumstances were always adverse
But now they're getting only worse and worse

The hearts in love are in a mess indeed
They ache and ache, and bleed and bleed

And love is an ailment totally obscure
There's no treatment; there's no cure

The pain and suffering do never cease
And even in heaven there is no peace

A loving heart is beyond repair
And, KHUSRO, in love there's only despair

181 Baaz gul bashguft o gulrooyaan soo e bustaan shudand

The spring is here with great fanfare
There're flowers and music, and girls everywhere

But seeing it came to me as a blow
That my gal was there with my terrible foe

And with birds so happy and flowers so gay
I could hardly contain my great dismay

So a man can't play a lover's part
Without first eating out his heart

But, KHUSRO, still if I cannot have girls
I can surely be happy thinking of their curls

182 Dil zay dast e mun baraft o aarzoo e dil bamaand

She took my heart but left the desire
Now only she can put out the fire

I still have sorrow; I still have pain
And I'm not allowed to even complain

But she can come and end the strife
And with a single look she can take my life

And if she does so, when I depart
She won't have to bother about my heart

And though it'll wander in her neighborhood
To my crazy heart it'll do no good

Then, KHUSRO, it will come back to me
And we'll both live forever in harmony

183 Raftiam az chashm o dar dil hasrat e rooyat bamaand

You may be gone but I see everywhere
Your lips, your eyes, your brow, your hair

From you, my love, if I have to part
I can drag my body but never my heart

O you're my predator, and I your prey
So come to your lover if only to slay

Your look is a dart; come throw it now
And for it you use the bow of your brow

Or come with your hair flying in the air
And use your curls your lover to snare

And though KHUSRO thinks it's all so crappy
Without you, darling, I can never be happy

184 Zhaala az nargis farobaareed o gul ra aab daad

When tears I see in my baby's eye
I feel as if I'm going to die

And when I see her long eyelashes
In my heart I get a million slashes

And when she looks, she throws a dart
That stabs and goes through my heart

And in her brow a bow I see
Aiming an arrow right at me

185 Bar bunagooshat bala e khat keh sar bar meekunad

Around neck and ears when gems you wear
You look like Venus with stars everywhere

And in the garden if you happen to be
You look like a graceful cypress tree

And when I wait and you do not come
I feel so stupid; I feel so dumb

And me when you appear not to know
It only encourages my terrible foe

And my love for you when you do not buy
I feel as if I'm going to die

And in your absence when I cry and cry
Says KHUSRO, I'm not the only guy

186 Jaan keh chu to dushmanay ra doostdaari meekunad

O she's the predator; I'm the prey
With blood in tears she makes me pay

She gives me sorrow; she gives me pain
And I bleed and bleed but cannot complain

Yes, I'm a victim of her dreamy eyes
The eyes that charm and terrorize

And in her street when I go and cry
She doesn't even look and passes by

But being there I so much prize
That in its dirt I rub my eyes

In sum, my predator I so much adore
That no idolater can worship her more

187   Baaz Turk e mast e mun aahang e baazi meekunad

My Turko girl, she plays with me
A flirt she is and will always be

She traps her lover in her raven hair
Her every lock is a deadly snare

And oh, her beautiful brown eyes
They charm, they enchant, they mesmerize

And her long eyelashes, they crucify
They make you bleed, and cry, and cry

And KHUSRO she can easily slay
She looks at him and he becomes her prey

188   Dil keh baa khoobaan e badkhoo aashnaaie meekunad

O why must we love a callous doll
And hit our heads against the wall?

We go for the girls who're insincere
And the cruel ones we hold so dear

And all lifelong for them we long
Knowing that to us they'll never belong

But when they smile, we're easily misled
And even the preacher loses his head

And even our KHUSRO who's so very smart
He also adores them with all his heart

189   Az dil e ghamgeen, hawa e dilsitaanam chun rawad

My heart her yearning will never leave
O it's all so crazy, and hard to believe

I had no problem when I was young
Now weak and old, I'm deeply stung

Oh, I'm a victim of her deadly dart
That, having struck, has stayed in my heart

My poor little heart does bleed and bleed
For the wounds it's caused are deep indeed

And when I'll be dying of my bleeding heart
Her dart from my heart will never part

And even when lying dead in my grave
My bones for her will always crave

In the meantime, KHUSRO, I'll cry and cry
And keep her image in my tearful eye

190   Ger kuni yaari o ger aazaar, bar mun bagzarad

The pain of a lover nothing can ease
So it doesn't matter, do as you please

I want you to be nice, yes it's true
But if it cannot be, it's all right too

All night long oh, how do I cry
My yearnings, I'm sure, will never die

And even when dead, I'll crave and crave
And hope someday you'll come to my grave

I've lost my mind; I've become insane
And I'm a lover that people disdain

For about my love they talk and talk
And me, O KHUSRO, they all love to mock

191 Mun nameekhaaham keh chashmam ghair e aan roo bangarad

To see her face they all so try
May God protect her from the evil eye

It's like a bow, her beautiful brow
And with it she kills her prey and how!

The moon is jealous of her beauty and grace
And the breeze is always kissing her face

And our KHUSRO also does his bit
And uses her picture as an amulet

192 Dast e maah e rooza ta dar chashm e ishrat khaak zad

A full month of fasting is very, very hard
These flowers and wine you can't disregard

And look how the garden is full of gloom
The flowers are sad and refuse to bloom

The tulips and roses are lying in the dust
So do be careful, if walk you must

The people in the pub are feeling all blue
And the maids of the bar have nothing to do

But lose not hope, for it'll be soon
That, KHUSRO, you'll see the new moon

193   Ta saram baashad tamanna e to am dar sar bawad

All lifelong I'll yearn and yearn
In the fire of love I'll totally burn

Her curly hair when it flies in the air
My consuming passion I cannot bear

And even in Heaven I'll feel her need
And my poor little heart will bleed and bleed

When I think of her I feel aflame
For I'm the moth and she's the flame

And when I'm burning in my flaming desire
I use my tears to put out the fire

I wish one day she'd come to me
And, KHUSRO, relieve this agony

194   Farrukh aan eiday keh jaan qurbaani e jaanaan bawad

At the altar of my goddess I offer my soul
For she is my object and my only goal

And the offering of mine if she would take
For her, what I have, I'll gladly forsake

But she is a coquette and a great flirt
And your creed and morals she can easily subvert

Her red, red lips are juicy and sweet
And listening to her is a wonderful treat

And when she wants to take your life
She needs no sword; she needs no knife

So, KHUSRO my friend, it's a great pleasure
To give up for her whatever you treasure

195 Zulf gird aawar keh baazam dil pareeshaan meeshawad

My heart does leap when it sees her curls
It jumps, and vaults, and whirls, and twirls

It gets so dazzled when it sees her face
That sense it loses of time and space

Her cruelties all it forgets outright
If appears she even slightly contrite

And if she ever comes to slay
My heart so loves to become her prey

But when preacher tries to give advice
It does not think that he's being nice

And when KHUSRO says that the girls are bad
It thinks it's crazy; he must be mad

196 Ta Khayaal e roo e aan shum e shabistaan deeda shud

Since that face I've come to admire
Like moth I'm burning in the flame of desire

O it's so radiant; it's so bright
That become it has the source of my light

So slim, and trim, and elegant is she
That shame she does every cypress tree

And when they see her lovers cry
They all want to see her, even passersby

And since he's heard of her charm and grace
Even KHUSRO is begging for a glimpse of her face

197   Baaz baad e subhay boo e aashnaaie meedahad

When the scent of her hair does bring the breeze
It puts the hearts of her lovers at ease

And when her curls do fly in the air
Their scent and fragrance is there everywhere

Her locks, her brow, her lips, her eyes
Her lovers adore and idolize

And to catch a glimpse of the face they adore
Like beggars they go and knock at her door

But all their pleas she does ignore
And treats them as aliens as never before

And tells them, KHUSRO, they make her ill
And that all of them she would like to kill

198   Gham makhur, aey dil, keh baaz ayyaam e shaadi hum rasad

I'm sick of sorrow; I'm sick of pain
If only some respite I could obtain

I do have wish; I do have desire
But a little bit of joy I also require

When creatures all from them are free
Why man is subject to sorrow and glee?

And I find it very hard to explain
Why the world is full of such sorrow and pain?

And why am I glum and so very sad
When others are happy and look so glad?

So, KHUSRO, please do pray for me
For only God can give me a little glee

199 Khabram shudaast kamshab sar e yaar khaahi aamad

Rejoice, O heart, she's coming tonight
And bringing with her a lot of moonlight

The night is dark without her moon
With a little bit of luck she might come soon

There's nothing like love but it takes its toll
It bleeds your heart and wounds your soul

In love you yearn, you crave, you pine
Its cup has blood instead of the wine

For love is a game, not a fair play
Your gal is a hunter and you're the prey

So, KHUSRO, you'll cry when she's away
But when she comes, she'll come to slay

200 Guzarad mahay o yak shab ba munat guzar na baashad

To see her moon you wait all night
And wait and wait and see no light

And when it's there in the sky at night
Even moon looks dark without her light

But it has so much beauty and grace
That you always want to look at her face

And what she says is so very sweet
That listening to her is always a treat

But when she comes and talks to you
You know not what to say or do

So it's not that easy, and loving her
Is not a job for an amateur

And, KHUSRO, this yearning is bound to recur
Because you're always thinking of her

201 To zay lab sukhan kushaadi, hama khalq baizabaan shud

O when she talks, you may not speak
She likes her lovers all weak and meek

And when she is walking in her street
She likes you to kiss the dirt of her feet

And of her twisted raven hair
She wants you to fall in a deadly snare

And her ruby lips and brown eyes
She wants you to adore and idolize

So, KHUSRO, her beauty you can only admire
But express you dare not your heart's desire

202 Dilberaan mehr numaayand o wafa neez kunand

O if she wants, she can be nice
And make this world a paradise

And though we often like to complain
Her friends and lovers we always remain

A foe not always acts like a foe
And a hunter sometimes lets you go

And though what's written you cannot prevent
Your fate sometimes does also relent

And though the rich do often ignore
They sometimes pity and help the poor

So, KHUSRO, the beauties are cruel and cold
But sometimes one has the heart of gold

203   Rasm e khoonraiz dar aan khoo e jafasaaz bamaand

May she always prey and slay
May she always be proud and gay

And the one she killed with a deadly glance
May she never forget that hapless prey

And she, who's slim like a cypress tree
May she never lose her swing and sway

And the watchful eyes that wait for her
May they forever stay that way

And the preacher, who seems immune to her
May he also become one day her prey

And our KHUSRO, who is in love with her
May he always cry and feel dismay

204   Bar rukh e humchu mehash turra e chu shab nigreed

Her ruby lips, so juicy and sweet
Her raven curls, so lovely and neat

And like an arch is her beautiful brow
The faithful to which all gladly bow

And like a trap is her dimpled chin
The lovers in it fall again and again

Her long eyelashes are like the darts
With which she stabs and wounds the hearts

And she herself is like a flower
With all its beauty, charm and power

And KHUSRO, when he writes his verse
He calls her the queen of the universe

205 Rooyat az ghaalia khat bar rukh e gulfaam kasheed

It shames the flowers, your beautiful face
And even the moon does feel disgrace

And tulip, when it tries to look like you
The birds and the bees all jeer and boo

And you at night do bring daylight
And without you day is darker than night

And when you come, and I'm feeling low
I forget my sorrow, my pain, my woe

So come, my darling, and be with me
And a happy lover O let me be

And KHUSRO says though love has pain
It also has joy, so you can't complain

206 Her shab az seena e mun teer e bala meeguzarad

This love, my darling, is madness pure
You don't know what I have to endure

I cry, and sigh, and moan, and groan
I'm made of flesh and not of stone

All night long I wait and wait
And pray to God and curse my fate

And if I'm lucky, the morning air
Brings with it the scent of your hair

It also stokes my fire of love
Which envy the lovebirds flying above

But KHUSRO says this too shall pass
And I'll get out of this morass

207 Shab, zay soazay keh bar een jaan e hazeen meeguzarad

Oh, the pain and sorrow she makes you bear
It can make your life a nightmare

And even the preacher who is a recluse
Whenever she wants, she can easily seduce

And also the moon, when it sees her at night
Thinks she is the source of all its light

And the breeze, when drunk with the scent of her hair
Whatever may happen it does not care

And even KHUSRO when she does mistreat
He simply surrenders, and kisses her feet

208 Aan keh her shab ba dilam aayad o jaay bakunad

She, who has me in her snare
For me, her lover, what does she care?

And when this prey she comes to slay
There's nothing I can do except to pray

Oh, how I hate my sorry state
And how I swear, and curse my fate

I wish she weren't as cruel and cold
And had some pity for her lover old

So, KHUSRO, now I sit and cry
Change her I cannot; I don't even try

209 Ger dil e aashiqam az ishq e to ranjoor shawad

This love has made my heart so sick
That it's now become a lunatic

But when I see her, even at night
She fills my heart and soul with light

And when she looks, her dreamy eyes
They intoxicate; they hypnotize

And when she gives me a beautiful smile
Her red, red lips, oh, how they beguile

And when I see her radiant face
In it I see the Divine grace

So, KHUSRO, you see, she's completely divine
And I only wish she could be mine

210 Mast e mun baikhabar az bazm chun dar khaana shawad

O come and fill my cup of wine
I'm in love with a dame divine

Her lovely glance is like a dart
It's terribly wounded my poor little heart

And though she's the hunter and I'm the prey
She becomes so friendly when she comes to slay

But her for burning I do not blame
For I'm the moth and she's the flame

And when I see her curly hair
My pangs of love I cannot bear

And in seclusion when I drink the wine
I see in it her image divine

Thus I can, KHUSRO, go on and on
But please forgive me if I make you yawn

211 Ger sar e zulf e to az baad pareeshaan nashawad

O if her curls didn't fly in the air
This love would've been easier to bear

On my faithful heart that infidel
Oh, how she casts her deadly spell

So I keep telling my silly little heart
That if not careful, she'll take it apart

But it's not she who is at fault
It's that beauty that we so exalt

So when they wonder why I love her so
I wonder how they can resist this doe

For, KHUSRO, my heart is like a fawn
It cannot resist; it feels so drawn

212 Aashiqay ra keh gham e doost beh az jaan nabawad

Love you don't if you don't love pain
And if you do, you wouldn't complain

The fire of love you cannot survive
And like a Hindu you'll burn alive

And if your sorrow does greatly increase
You'll take the poison and die in peace

You may be faithful but she's a belle
So completely faithless, such infidel

She also has beauty, charm, and grace
And everybody loves her gorgeous face

And, KHUSRO you're a nightingale
You are born to love, and wail, and wail

213 Mard e sahibnazar az koo e to aasaan narawad

Her lovers are never very far away
Close to her they all want to stay

In the hope their gal they might meet
All day, all night they wait in her street

And of her presence they're acutely aware
For in their hearts she's always there

She is their goddess of love, of course
Of the spring of life she's the source

And she is also a beautiful flower
And everything in the garden is in her power

And KHUSRO, because she is so pretty
He is also stuck in Delhi, her city

214 To keh roozat ba nishaat e dil o jaan meeguzarad

Oh, when she comes and doesn't say hi
I just can't help it, I cry and cry

And in my tears I shed my blood
And weep so much, I cause a flood

And though her glance is like a dart
By not looking also she wounds my heart

And when she tries on others her dart
It bleeds and bleeds, my poor little heart

So then it goes and lies in her street
And hopes to become the dirt of her feet

But KHUSRO says it's no use to cry
On moaning and groaning I shouldn't rely

215   Ya Rab, een shohra e lashkar zay kuja meeaayad

This Turko girl wherever she goes
She brings to lovers a host of woes

And cruel are her beautiful eyes
The hearts they maul and traumatize

And brings when air the scent of her hair
It only increases the lovers' despair

They are not looking for mirth or glee
They merely want some sympathy

Her smiling face, so when they see
They cannot contain their ecstasy

And KHUSRO says, it's all in the game
And her for it they cannot blame

216   Sabzaha meedamad o aab e rawaan meeaayad

O when they see my tearful eye
The clouds in heaven, they start to cry

It's green and lush with spring in the air
And the people are falling in love everywhere

With the trees and bushes so green and gay
My cypress O why she's so far away?

So in this beautiful atmosphere
I wait and wait for her to appear

And may be God will grant my prayer
And the breeze will bring the scent of her hair

But because I'm dying to see her face
I'm always going from place to place

For, KHUSRO, my heart is like a steed
It is totally out of control indeed

217 Een chuneen tund keh aan qalbshikan meeaayad

O even when she is nice to me
Expect I cannot any sympathy

And even when she is trying to flirt
A loving heart she can easily hurt

Oh, she's a coquette, cagey and sly
And a beautiful, beautiful butterfly

So even when lying dead in the grave
Her lovers' hearts do crave and crave

And even our KHUSRO, the poet great
Resist he cannot her beautiful bait

218 Gercheh dar kushtan e ushshaaq zaboon meeaayad

No matter how much she feels contrite
Preying and slaying are always all right

And no matter how much her lovers complain
She says their fate is to suffer the pain

And no matter how much her victims cry
She thinks her preys she must crucify

And shedding tears though they cannot stop
Her image they see in every little drop

And no matter how much sorrow they bear
Of her scented curls they love the snare

They cannot forget her dreamy eyes
And how they enchant and mesmerize

And remember they also KHUSRO's advice
That those who love must pay the price

219 Khashmgeen yaar e mara dil ba raza baaz aamad

Come, my love, don't be so severe
When did I say you're not sincere?

Yes, you can be quite cruel and cold
But then you've also a heart of gold

So come, my dear, do come to me
And if you can't be nice, just let it be

That you will come I pray and pray
Although in it I have no say

I have lost my heart; I've lost my mind
And neither of them will I ever find

But then there's no one that I can blame
For, as KHUSRO says, it's all in the game

220 Her kasay gaah e jawaani tag o pooay daarad

In youth the heart is beyond control
In the garden of love it loves to stroll

In the twists and turns of the raven hair
It loves to be caught in a lovely snare

And a Turko girl it wants to meet
And become the lowly dirt of her feet

It wants to spend the rest of his life
With a lovely, lovely, beautiful wife

And though KHUSRO says that beauty is cold
Onto it tight he's so eager to hold

221 Aey, keh az khaak e darat deeda munawwar gardad

His eyes love the dirt of your feet
And needs his soul your fragrance sweet

Oh, away from them he cannot keep
Let him kiss your feet and weep and weep

And use your brow to throw a dart
And jab, and stab, and wound his heart

He wants you to come and take his life
And not to be shy of using your knife

Like daggers are your long eyelashes
With them you can kill with a few good slashes

So to his pleas O please do heed
And stab your KHUSRO and let him bleed

222 Waqtay aan kaafir e bai rehm az aan e mun bood

O how I love that infidel
Though she has made my life hell

All night long I gasp and sigh
And like a candle I burn and cry

My life is hard; I'm in a bind
I've lost my heart; I've lost my mind

I've lost my color; I've become so pale
So lean and thin; so weak and frail

And she is a coquette, cagey and coy
And causing trouble she does enjoy

And she's made me a laughing stock
That everyone, KHUSRO, likes to mock

223   Jaan fida e pisaraanay keh nikooroo baashand

Oh, how I love that beautiful doe
Cruel and callous she is although

Her gorgeous face I love to see
Although she drives me up the tree

O she can kill you with a single glance
And when she hunts, you don't have a chance

So when you love such an infidel
You lose your creed; you go to hell

But even KHUSRO who's a poet great
To become her victim he cannot wait

224   Yaar e zaiba e mara baaz ba mun banmaayeed

My sweetie little pie O let me see
That pretty butterfly O let me see

That gal who makes me bleed and bleed
And for whom I die O let me see

My moon who makes the night so bright
That pie in the sky O let me see

The babe who robs and plunders the heart
And loves to crucify O let me see

The lass who leaves me and goes away
And calls me her guy O let me see

And the sugar who makes the life so sweet
That apple of my eye O let me see

225 Yaar baaz aamad o boo e gul o reehaan aawurd

I see in them my sweetie pie
These flowers make me cry and cry

When a budding rose in them I see
It reminds me so much of her modesty

While everyone rejoices in the spring
Only sorrow to me oh, it does bring

So in the spring I sigh and sob
And my fire makes my heart a kabob

Tree after tree in the park I see
But see I do not my cypress tree

So I start to pray that she'd come
And make my life less burdensome

And bring she would her deadly dart
And jab and stab her KHUSRO's heart

226 Her keh ra yaaray chu to sarkash bawad

A man whose gal is a willful shrew
With happiness he is forever through

But her for burning he cannot blame
For he is the moth and she's the flame

Her hapless lover she'll always mistreat
And think that he's the dirt of her feet

And if, while kissing, he bites her lip
O him forever she'll rip and whip

And, KHUSRO, she will not let him complain
He'll have to endure the sorrow and pain

227   Laal e sheereenay chun khandaan meeshawad

Her lovers, whenever they see her smile
Their pangs of love all become worthwhile

And when in the park she takes a walk
The cypress trees all begin to rock

And with her rosy, radiant cheek
She makes the sun and moon look bleak

And when her curls do fly in the air
Their passion for her the lovers can't bear

And when they see her gorgeous face
They lose their sense of time and space

And when KHUSRO comes and sings her praise
He sets the hearts of her lovers ablaze

228   Dilam az bakht gahay shaad nabood

This love has brought me nothing but pain
The bondage now has become a bane

It's now a burden, an albatross
My life is nothing but a total loss

Its fire has burnt my heart entire
In which there's nothing but a dead desire

Of nothing in life I'm now aware
Except that in it she once was there

In a beautiful garden I used to be
Where she was a lovely cypress tree

And though a bondage was love to me
I was so very happy in captivity

But, KHUSRO, though she's still very sweet
My life has become a wreck complete

229 Ger sukhan zaan lab e chu noosh shawad

Oh, when she opens her luscious lips
With every word much honey drips

And seeing her teeth is a pure delight
They look like pearls, all white and bright

And the moon when it sees her gorgeous face
It can't help feeling so commonplace

And if she gives them poison to drink
They are drinking syrup, her lovers think

And of her twisted raven hair
They love to be caught in a deadly snare

And when she smiles, she can simply disarm
And even KHUSRO cannot resist her charm

230 Ger jaam e gham farasti, noasham keh gham na baashad

It's hard to take, this sorrow of mine
Would someone please bring me some wine?

Her image is always before my eye
And it will be there until I die

Like daggers are her long eyelashes
With them oh, how my heart she slashes

She stabs me deep with a deadly dagger
And then she mocks me when I stagger

This constant strife I cannot face
O take me please to a peaceful place

For love, O KHUSRO, is like a bog
I'm stuck and mired, and sick like a dog

231   Sarvay chu qaamat e to dar boostaan nabaashad

Like you, my love, it's clear to me
Is slim and trim no cypress tree

Your beautiful eyes, they throw the darts
And right and left they wound the hearts

And the way you wink and the way you glance
You make your lovers all go in a trance

And even our KHUSRO begins to coo
And cannot hide his love for you

232   Ma ra zay koo e jaanaan azm e safar nabaashad

O I feel so happy in her street
For there I find my only retreat

Of her sugary mouth whenever I talk
I can talk and talk around the clock

But for my rival I only have scorn
For she is a rose and he is a thorn

And he has fun, that miserable guy
When I sit, and wait, and sob, and cry

But in her presence I make no scene
For I'm a beggar and she is the queen

So, KHUSRO, her I can never reach
And there's no way I can close the breach

233   Dee mast booda am keh zay khaisham khabar nabood

O where am I, I do not know
I can't even tell a friend from a foe

Of all my despair though she's aware
What happens to me she doesn't really care

My crazy heart I cannot rein
This love is driving me insane

Very cold and callous I've now become
Do please forgive me, I'm totally numb

I also don't care, because I suppose
I've gotten used to my troubles and woes

And, KHUSRO, I do not even remember
Whether it is April, June, or December

234   Yaaray keh bar judaaie e oyam gumaan nabood

When she and I were so very close
Why did she leave, only Heaven knows?

Yes, she left me just like that
No feud, no fight, not even a spat

I was her lover; I was her beau
There was no rival; there was no foe

With all these flowers now everywhere
To leave a lover is not very fair

I still have hope that she'll be back
Although it all looks so very black

And KHUSRO says I shouldn't despair
For winter is never forever there

235   Dee zakhm e naakhunash ba rukh e chu saman cheh bood

Your luscious red lips O who did bite
And rumple your hair who did last night?

Some terrible sorrow they do disguise
O whatever happened to your starry eyes?

What did you do with your deadly darts
That used to jab and wound the hearts?

Hunting and slaying O when did you quit
Your thirst for blood, what happened to it?

You used to kill and bury the dead
And your ill-repute you used to dread

Says KHUSRO, again you take control
And come and kill him body and soul

236   Dil dar hawayat, aey but e ayyaar, jaan dahad

O live I cannot away from you
Without you, darling, I feel so blue

I miss the scent of your curly hair
For the musk and incense I do not care

I miss your eyes; I miss your brow
Your long eyelashes I miss and how

Those ruby lips, O how I miss
And how that mouth I'm dying to kiss

And how I love the way you walk
And the way like cypress you sway and rock

And the way on KHUSRO you use your eyes
To charm, and enchant, and mesmerize

237 Baaz aan sawaar e mast ba nakhcheer meerawad

O the way she rides her white steed
She makes her lovers her slaves indeed

And when she uses the bow of her brow
Her fallen lovers, they all say wow!

And when their lonely hearts she breaks
Oh, what a horrible mess she makes

Her gaze is like a deadly dart
It jabs, and stabs, and wounds the heart

And her curly, twisted raven hair
It's a mortal trap and a deadly snare

So when our KHUSRO she makes her prey
The people all over, they say hurray!

238 Kaaraest dar saram keh ba samaan nameerasad

For the pangs of love there's no cure
O it's an ailment you must endure

Yes, it's a defect you cannot mend
The madness of love does never end

When I beg and beg and she comes to me
I get so dazzled, I cannot see

With a single look she can cause a blight
And feel she does not at all contrite

But my heart is a faithless infidel
And she's its idol, that beautiful belle

And, KHUSRO, it's also an amateur
And stop it you cannot from loving her

239 Bar mun kunoon keh bai to jahaan teerafaam shud

Without her face is dark my night
And even the day is without any light

All night long she sleeps so tight
When awake I lie in bed all night

The birds all sing and fly in the air
But stay I captive, caught in a snare

She's proud and happy, and the way she behaves
Even kings, she makes them feel like slaves

And the lovers who want to see her face
She makes them feel all low and base

And even KHUSRO she rides like a steed
And he has to submit and obey indeed

240 Yaaray kash az karishma o khoobi nishaan bawad

The gal I love is a beautiful lass
But cruel is she and cold, alas!

O I'm her lover, her nightingale
And she's my rose, and for her I wail

Her gorgeous face I want to see
But keeps she always away from me

And though I can speak and I can sway
I just can't tell her what I want to say

So to say – I love her – I don't even try
And sit all night and cry and cry

But, KHUSRO, I wish, and hope, and pray
That away from me she wouldn't always stay

241 Turkay o khoobrooay kasay keen chuneen bawad

My Turko girl who looks so smart
Inside she has a stony heart

She has every night a pleasant dream
But when I dream, it makes me scream

With a sword in hand when she comes to slay
Her lovers instantly become her prey

But when she comes with a flask of wine
Even the preachers say that she's divine

And when she speaks, and parts her lips
From them all over only honey drips

So, KHUSRO, you see wherever she goes
She brings to her lovers only troubles and woes

242 Shoakhi nigar keh aan but e ayyaar meekunad

She is so very smart, that maiden fair
Her lover she binds with her braided hair

And then with all the visible splendor
She makes him yield; she makes him surrender

And like a rose she shows her scorn
By favoring his rival, that prickly thorn

She makes him suffer the public disgrace
When she treats her lover as low and base

And she also makes him look so grim
That even our preacher feels sorry for him

And so in short, it's needless to say
That the smartest of men she can make her prey

And that when he sees her, he starts to croon
For to her even KHUSRO in not so immune

243   Chun aan but az sar e koo baa hazaar naaz aayad

O when she walks with pomp and pride
Their love for her the lovers can't hide

Oh, how she makes them cry and cry
May God protect her from the evil eye

Their blood in tears but when they shed
Hurting her feeling, oh, how they dread

Her gorgeous face they cannot forget
For they love so much their Juliet

And that she's divine they all concur
So like a goddess they worship her

244   Chun Turk e mast e mun aalooda e sharaab daraayad

My Turko girl, when she drinks some wine
Her lovely face, it becomes divine

But when that face I want to kiss
She tells me no with an emphasis

Her long eyelash is like a dart
It sets it on fire, my peaceful heart

Her raven tress is like a snare
It catches my heart and keeps it there

And when she leaves, she makes me cry
And loves the blood I shed from my eye

245   Mahay guzisht keh chashmam
khabar zay khaab na daarad

Her absence has turned me into a loon
For I cannot sleep without her moon

I don't want to live; I'd like to die
Because when dead, I won't have to cry

Her moon does brighten my rival's night
While dark is my day without her light

She tells me I can see her in my dream
But I've insomnia, and it is extreme

I've lost my patience; I've lost my mind
My heart is crazy; I'm in a bind

And, KHUSRO my friend, I've become so weak
That when she's there, I can't even speak

246   Zay gusht mast raseed o ba housh e khaish na bood

O you'll be dazzled when you see her face
It has such beauty, and charm, and grace

When she looks at you, she throws a dart
That hits and jabs and stabs the heart

And if you've seen her, you'll concur
That she makes you fall in love with her

And though he poses as a moralist
Her even the preacher, he cannot resist

But, KHUSRO, to me it's also quite plain
That you cannot love her without the pain

247 Mahay bar aamad o az maah e mun khabar naraseed

The night is moonless without your moon
So come back, darling, and come back soon

I've a feeling, you're having an affair
For there must be something keeping you there

And there you're having a time swell
While here I'm burning in the fire of hell

And I get the feeling, my beautiful friend
That the pain of your absence will never end

And in this our KHUSRO concurs with me
And thinks you again I will never see

248 Gul raseed o her kasay soo e gulistaan meerawad

With flowers, they say, they want to be
But they go to the garden their gal to see

Where, when they see her taking a stroll
On their loving hearts they lose control

So among the flowers when she takes a walk
They all sit there and gawk and gawk

And when she's there, it looks so nice
That they say by God it's paradise

And they find themselves in such a state
That they try and cannot walk straight

Yes, KHUSRO, it sounds rather bizarre
But that's the way the lovers are

249 Dil e mara chun zay roo e to yaad meeaayad

Whenever, my love, I think of you
I'm not only happy, but also blue

But you're now proud to such a degree
That you even do not remember me

O in my heart you have lit a fire
That, if not quenched, it'll burn me entire

Now every morning I wait for the air
To bring me the scent of your raven hair

And I remain your KHUSRO who loves you so
So come back to him, and don't say no

250 Bia nazaara kun, aey dil, keh yaar meeaayad

Rejoice, O heart, she'll soon be here
To rob you again and again, my dear

And she'll be coming on a white steed
Followed by lovers, in full speed

And when she comes, she'll be happily drunk
So get you ready for her, you punk

But when you see her, don't ever lust
For she'll reduce you to a speck of dust

And get you ready to wail and wail
For KHUSRO says, you're a nightingale

251 Sapeedadam keh jahaanay zay khaab bar khaizad

The sun is burning the veil of night
And waking us all from a slumber tight

It is also telling the morning breeze
The tulips and roses to go and tease

The sky in the east is all on fire
While the dawn is coming, playing its lyre

So it's now time for the topers to rise
And go to the bar and to socialize

And for the maids to rise and shine
And serve the topers with the morning wine

For soon the king will also be up
And is going to ask for his golden cup

Then also will come our KHUSRO, the slob
Looking for his liquor and shish kabob

252 Dilay keh nargis e mastash ba naaz bastaanad

Her charming eye, when it throws a dart
It jabs, and stabs, and wounds the heart

And when she holds a glass of wine
The wine in it, she makes it shine

And when sometimes she sees me cry
She comes and kisses my tearful eye

But then she kills me without delay
For she's the huntress and I the prey

And she also gives me a lot of pain
Which, KHUSRO, I think is all in vain

253 Kidaam shab keh tura dar kinaar khaaham kard

O let me, darling, hold you tight
And please, for God's sake, do not fight

And at your feet when I put my heart
O don't be angry, and don't be tart

And if it bleeds under your feet
O say you not, it's indiscreet

And when it gives a cry of pain
O scold it not and do not disdain

And if it declares its love for you
Then let it love; then let it woo

254 Ba bakht e aan keh ba moo e to raah khaaham kerd

My pain and sorrow I try to mention
In order to get a little attention

But when she doesn't believe my story
I try to talk of her grace and glory

I tell her she's an aristocrat
And praise a lot her stylish hat

But when I do not get very far
I simply go to the nearest bar

And there to the maids I tell my woe
And my wounded heart I try to show

I try to detail my terrible blight
And that's how, KHUSRO, I spend my night

255 Agercheh baa to hadees e jafa bakhaaham kerd

To her although I might complain
In love with her I'll always remain

And yes, I have been through a lot
But do without her I just cannot

Her ruby lips I like to kiss
But like she does not my doing this

And if her lips I sometimes bite
She wants to kick me or kill outright

And though in so much we don't concur
She remains my goddess, and I worship her

For her beautiful face I'm willing to die
May God protect her from the evil eye

So, KHUSRO, I love her with all my soul
And this is something I cannot control

256 Shab ooftaad o ghamam baaz kaar khaahad kerd

More sorrow and pain I just can't take
I'm afraid, one day I'm going to break

And with my rival I don't want to fight
For he is a dog, and he can bite

And if she's a rose, he is a thorn
Which makes me feel very forlorn

So when I think of my sweetie pie
I lose my patience and start to cry

In what she does, I have no voice
For I'm her slave as a matter of choice

But KHUSRO says, though I'm weak
I shouldn't appear to be so meek

257 Munam keh ta ziam az ishq mast khaaham bood

O drunk with love I choose to be
And beauty is what I love to see

To sense and reason I've said adieu
Now drinking my wine is all I do

I go in a trance and whirl and twirl
And worship I only my beautiful girl

In love I find my joy and glee
And happy is what I want to be

And when God was making the heaven and earth
He gave me, KHUSRO, only love and mirth

258 Saba zay zulf e to booay ba aashiqaan aawurd

When brought the breeze the scent of her hair
All the broken hearts it did repair

May God Almighty bless the breeze
For putting the hearts of her lovers at ease

But when it was playing with her curly hair
It saw my heart caught in a snare

Oh, it was weeping, and chanting her name
And saying, for its plight it's only to blame

Without her, it said, it could not stay
So became it her captive right away

And, KHUSRO, now to her it prays
For she is the goddess, and her it obeys

259 Chun khat e sabz e to bar aaftaab banweesad

Her cheek is like the sun at noon
Her curls are clouds covering her moon

And when red wine in a cup I sip
I think I'm kissing her ruby lip

But see when clouds my tearful eye
They feel so sorry, they start to cry

And when they see me sob and sigh
They all feel grieved, the stars in sky

And my blood in tears when sees the king
To cheer me, KHUSRO, he will do anything

260 Dar to kasaanay keh nazar meekunand

O those who see her lovely mole
Their loving hearts they cannot control

And those who kiss the dirt of her feet
They're all considered the real elite

And those who smell her fragrant hair
They do not care for the morning air

And those to whom she gives a smile
They become the slaves of its lovely guile

And when the preachers their love deplore
Their silly scolding they learn to ignore

So when you see her being idolized
You shouldn't be, KHUSRO, at all surprised

261 Mager fitna e ishq baidaar shud

It's time to love, the topers say
They're going to the bar to drink and play

The barman is asking that they feel free
To sell their creed and piety

And to buy and drink the heady wine
That'll make them have the vision divine

And though love's great; it's also hard
For pain and sorrow you can't disregard

So when in love, you'll cry and cry
And moan, and groan, and sob, and sigh

And when in love with the curly hair
You're bound to be caught in its deadly snare

And says our KHUSRO, the great expert
That beautiful girls do always flirt

262 Sabzaha nau dameed o yaar niyaamad

The flowers have come but she's not here
And without that gal there is no cheer

O of my doll what has become
To see the flowers she hasn't come?

We have in the garden tree after tree
But my graceful cypress I do not see

And though they do not lack in grace
The flowers are dying to see her face

But falling in love is not very smart
For you drink your blood and eat your heart

And, KHUSRO, though you may not complain
In love there's also a lot of pain

263 Ta tura jism o jaan shikaar bawad

She's the predator; you're the prey
She takes your heart and goes away

And though her lips are juicy and sweet
You're only allowed to kiss her feet

But if her lips you can ever kiss
Your ruby wine you'll never miss

An arch of prayer is her lovely brow
Even preacher to it does always bow

And if she gives you a lot of pain
You'll learn to love it and never complain

And, KHUSRO, her when you're going to meet
Worship her you will and kiss her feet

264 Paish e roo e to yaasmeen keh bawad

O she's like a flower, my baby bunny
And in her lips she has a lot of honey

She has a scent in her curly hair
To which no musk can ever compare

And she has also a gorgeous face
That's young and fresh and full of grace

A face that glows like the sun at noon
And is so much prettier than the harvest moon

So people for her do yearn and crave
And even our KHUSRO is her faithful slave

265   Her kira yaar yaar meeoftad

A man who becomes her bosom friend
To the seventh heaven he'll surely ascend

And a man who does for his baby cry
Everyone will kiss his tearful eye

And a man who's lured by her charming eye
He'll sit for ever and sob and sigh

And a man for her who's going to wail
He'll surely be called a nightingale

And a man who loves her eye's dart
He'll end up nursing a wounded heart

And a man who wants to become her prey
She'll love to catch him and quickly slay

And a man who becomes her faithful slave
Like KHUSRO he'll always yearn and crave

266   Dil zay roo e to dour natwaan kard

Your beautiful face I cannot forget
And do without you I can't, my pet

Your love has brought me a lot of pain
But I'm in love; I cannot complain

And whether it's wet or whether it's dry
Your image is always there in my eye

This being without you I cannot bear
Don't make me wait, it's so unfair

So come to your KHUSRO before it's night
His nights are dark without your light

267   Dilbaram baiwafaast chitwaan kard

O she's a coquette; she is a flirt
And someone like her you cannot convert

And when you're a slave and she the queen
Her, by loving, you can only demean

To the rules of love she doesn't adhere
And being a beauty, she is insincere

And what she tells you, is never true
And keeping a promise, she cannot do

She loves to give you sorrow and pain
And wouldn't allow you to even complain

She's always cruel; she's always cold
She loves to admonish; she loves to scold

She'll take your heart and say adieu
And care for you, she'll never do

So you can do, KHUSRO, only boohoo
For there's nothing else that you can do

268   Dil e baadard ra kuja yaaband

A kind heart, O where do you find
A heart that feels for the humankind?

Your grief and sorrow, they all subside
And you do feel better after you've cried

And when you look at the beautiful face
Your pain and sorrow it does erase

And when you receive some sympathy
You can cope much better with cruelty

So cope with pain as best you can
And when you die, you die like a man

And stay you, KHUSRO, out of the bog
And be a lion and not a dog

269   Shikan e zulf baaz khaahi kard

O do untie your knotted hair
And let your tresses fly in the air

And let me kiss your juicy lip
Its sugary nectar O let me sip

And let me worship and let me bow
To the arch of prayer that's your brow

And when I knock, do open your door
And let me kiss the dirt of your floor

And with your KHUSRO don't please be sore
For he's your lover, so meek, so poor

270   Labash dar shakarkhanda jaan meeburad

It robs your heart with its lovely guile
On her ruby lips that darling smile

And the way she carries the cups and wine
She makes her lovers all yearn and pine

And her golden belt the way she wears
It hits your heart which then despairs

And when her curls do cover her eyes
The loving hearts they so terrorize

O she's a beauty, so fresh, so young
On her the lovers are terribly hung

And all this, KHUSRO, is very hard to bear
And the lovers can only tear their hair

271 Hawa e khurramast o her taraf baaraan meebaarad

With drops of rain on every flower
It seems that the park is taking a shower

These drops of water look like the pearls
In the raven locks of the beautiful girls

With the girls all strolling and the lovers singing
The bees are buzzing and the birds are winging

And there to clean the beauties' path
The grass is also taking a bath

But in this garden there's also a guy
Who's missing his gal and wants to cry

And then there's KHUSRO telling everyone
To join the party and have some fun

272 Hawa e khurramast o abr e lulubaar meebaarad

The drops of rain are cooling the air
It's all so green and gay everywhere

There are flowers red, and blue, and white
And the birds are winging in great delight

The girls are also there everywhere
Looking all very chic and debonair

There're also guys watching the dames
With their yearning hearts all in flames

The flames of passion that without a doubt
No falling rain can ever put out

And the angels in heaven, seeing all this
Are envying KHUSRO for the earthly bliss

273 Khush aan shabay keh
saram zaer e pa e yaar bamaand

A man who kisses his baby's feet
He becomes a part of the real elite

And a man who loves the maid of the bar
Among the topers he becomes a star

And a man in love who goes in trance
He knows the meaning of the real romance

And a man who loves his lass' dart
He sits and nurses a wounded heart

And a man who loves to hear her talk
He does not care if the preachers mock

And a man who, KHUSRO, likes to complain
In pain forever he's bound to remain

274 Dil shud zay dast o bar
mizha az khoon nishaan bamaand

She took my heart and gave me pain
I lost my freedom and got a chain

The pang of love has taken its toll
It's become a thorn inside my soul

I get from friends a lot of advice
But this is not also without its price

The preachers, though they themselves drink
When they see me drinking, they make a stink

I've lost my heart; I'm losing my mind
This love is becoming a terrible grind

So, KHUSRO, all night I sit and cry
And moan, and groan, and sob, and sigh

275 Ushshaaq her shab az to ba khoonaab khufta and

Crying all night when I cannot keep
I get exhausted and fall asleep

But my darling girl, she sleeps all night
And does not bother about my plight

And my horrible foes, they're always glad
To see me crying and feeling sad

So they're very happy; they sleep till noon
While all night long I cry for the moon

For she like moon has a radiant face
So full of charm; so full of grace

In a moonlit night so if I cry
Ignore me, KHUSRO, and don't ask why?

276 Gercheh khoobaan zay meh fazoon baashand

She is slim, and trim, and smart, and tall
My doll is prettier than any other doll

So when they see her beauty and grace
Even kings and princes feel small and base

But she is a siren, a nymph indeed
And she wants your heart to bleed and bleed

And when she sips the ruby wine
She becomes a goddess and looks divine

And when to dance her robe she sheds
Even sheiks and mystics, they lose their heads

But someday, I hope, she will discover
That like her KHUSRO there is no lover

277   Yaaraan keh booda and, nadaanam kuja shudand

My loving friends, they all are gone
There is no one now to depend upon

O flower, tell me where are they
The beauties under the earth that lay?

And where are now the mighty kings
Who went to dust with all their things?

This world of ours is a terrible snare
For even the wisest get caught in there

So fall you not in this awful abyss
For you'll never have any peace or bliss

And if you, KHUSRO, fell in the pit
Don't ever expect any good from it

278   Aey ahl e dil, nakhist zay jaan tark e jaan kuneed

O if you want to love a dame
You should realize it's not a game

She'll make you into a slave complete
And ask you to kiss the dirt of her feet

Your blood one day she's going to shed
And through the city parade your head

She'll torch your soul, that infidel
And let it burn in the fire of hell

And in your heart she'll light a fire
And burn in it your every desire

Then your body charred she's going to save
And make it, KHUSRO, a branded slave

279 Chun baad e subhey baa aan sarv e khushkharaam shawad

When in the morning she takes a walk
With her, O breeze, you go and talk

Tell her, for her I yearn and crave
For since I saw her, I've become her slave

With the bow of her brow she's thrown a dart
That's hit, and jabbed, and stabbed my heart

And though she's cruel, and callous, and cold
On me she strictly maintains her hold

So me in her street whenever they see
Her neighbors, KHUSRO, feel sorry for me

280 Saba chun dar sar e aan zulf e neemtaab shawad

Seeing her curls flying in the air
For a hapless lover, it's hard to bear

In the twists and turns of her raven hair
A captive heart can only despair

And if you worship her rosy cheek
You're going to be surely up the creek

And if you love her almond eyes
You're going to be charmed before you realize

And kiss her month if you would dare
The spring of life you'll find in there

And if you would go to her door and knock
She will not answer; she will not talk

And if you would try to kiss her feet
She'll tell you, KHUSRO, you're indiscreet

281 Gham kusht mara, aan but e naushaad niyaamad

In pain I died but came she not
Oh, me, her lover, she simply forgot

A man who falls in love with her
From an ailment such he doesn't recover

And even when he goes into his grave
He craves for her, and remains her slave

And though she wouldn't tell him no
Having promised to come, she will not show

And if he sobs, and sighs, and cries
She will not care if he lives or dies

So, KHUSRO, though we hold them dear
The beauties by nature are insincere

282 Kidaam dil keh to ghamza zadi figaar nashud

Wherever you look there's a wounded heart
No heart's immune to her deadly dart

My cry of pain can melt a stone
But can't even touch her, my moan and groan

I knew one day she was going to depart
And the pain of parting would devour my heart

And now that the flowers are about to appear
My beautiful cypress will not be here

In fact, I know she'll never be mine
For I'm only human and she is divine

And one day, KHUSRO, she'll toll the bell
And burn me forever in the fire of hell

283 Kasay keh deedan e aan Turk e baadanoash rawad

Whoever sees her gorgeous face
Awed he is by its beauty and grace

By God she's a very beautiful dame
In charm and style she's made her name

And even the sheik, who's a moralist
Her beauty and style he cannot resist

So when for her I cry and cry
They all want to kiss my tearful eye

And a lot of nice things they say
For they want to see me happy and gay

But without her, KHUSRO, I cannot do
So I sigh, and cry, and do boohoo

284 Kasay keh deedan e aan chashm e khaabnaak rawad

Beware, friends, of her dreamy eyes
They charm, and enchant, and hypnotize

And of her juicy, red, red lips
Much honey from which forever drips

And of her lashes which like darts
So jab, and stab, and wound the hearts

And when she says to you good-bye
Cares she not if you sob and sigh

And in your heart she lights a fire
That burn in it your soul entire

So if you fall in love with her
KHUSRO, you know, you'll never recover

285 Hawaay dar saram uftaada, jaanam khaak khaahad shud

I love the way at me she winks
And her charming eyes the way she blinks

And the way she uses her eye's dart
To jab, and stab, and wound my heart

All night long I toss and turn
In the fire of love oh, how I burn

But her for burning I cannot blame
For I'm the moth and she's the flame

So when she sees my terrible plight
I don't want to see her feel contrite

Even her bitter words to me are sweet
And, KHUSRO, I do not mind the heat

286 Zay douri e to chun khoonaaba e mun afzoon shud

From my eyes when I shed my blood
I miss her so much, I cause a flood

I wail and wail, like a nightingale
And blood in my tears tells all my tale

But she's so splendid, proud and cold
That cares she not for a lover old

She robs her lover of his faith and creed
And loves to see him bleed and bleed

And, KHUSRO, his tears, she thinks, are pearls
With which to adorn her raven curls

287 Chun kushaadi dahaan e shakkarkhand

O when you part your ruby lips
Honey from them all over drips

So let me kiss that luscious lip
And all that honey O let me sip

O you're so gorgeous, my sweetie pie
May God protect you from the evil eye

You're tall and slim like a cypress tree
And at your feet I want to be

So come and throw your eye's dart
And jab, and stab, and wound my heart

And worry you not about my pain
For I'm your KHUSRO; I do not complain

288 Imroaz keh az baaraan shud sabza e raana tar

With rain the grass is green and lush
And the flowers have also a lot of flush

And because I miss my Juliet
With tears my eyes are also wet

So when I hear the sound of feet
I begin to hope that she's in the street

And with all the flowers all over the place
I begin to miss her beautiful face

Her brow, her eyes I also miss
And her ruby lips I want to kiss

And then I start to wail and wail
For, KHUSRO, I'm a nightingale

289   Aey, shum e rukh e to matla e noor

You're a beautiful, beautiful butterfly
May God protect you from the evil eye

When sees the moon your radiant face
It can't help feeling very low and base

For when your face does shine at night
It gives the moon and stars their light

Your raven hair is dark as night
But with your face the night gets bright

But then it is also quite plain
That loving you, darling, is full of pain

Even so, the man who loves your face
In flowers he finds no beauty and grace

And KHUSRO, your slave, does pray and pray
That far from him may you never stay

290   Aey, zay chu to but shuda sad paarsa zinnaardaar

For her there's no one who doesn't fall
Even sheiks and mystics, they worship my doll

I love so much my sorrow and pain
That when I'm happy, I start to complain

I wait and wait for her deadly dart
To jab, and stab, and wound my heart

I love my wound; I love my sore
For it reminds me of my predator

Yes, I'm her lover: I'm her slave
For her I'll always yearn and crave

My tears of blood I do not disguise
And on her feet I rub my eyes

And, KHUSRO, then I go in a trance
And lose myself and dance and dance

291 Ya Rab, aan rooyast ya gulberg e khandaan dar nazar

She's tall and slim like a cypress tree
With all its elegance and dignity

And like a flower is her lovely face
With all the beauty, and charm, and grace

And when in the park she takes a stroll
The birds in there all begin to troll

The night is dark without her light
And dark is even the moonlit night

And without the glow of her rosy cheek
The smiling flowers look all so bleak

292 Aey, tura dar zaer e her lab shakkaristaan e diger

With her luscious lips and mouth sweet
No honey and sugar can ever compete

But then she's also proud and vain
And shows contempt and great disdain

She'll come and steal your poor little heart
And piece by piece she'll take it apart

She'll have the power to give you life
And also to kill you without the knife

And being a beautiful infidel
She'll easily send you straight to hell

So if you want to be her lover
You must be willing to die for her

And, KHUSRO, you should also recognize
That you'll be bleeding from your eyes

293 Jolaan e tausanash been, her soo ghubaar e deeger

I wish she'd come, if only to slay
For I so love to be her prey

For her I pine, and yearn, and crave
For I'm her captive, an abject slave

I cannot forget her beautiful smile
Her poise and carriage, her chic style

Her luscious lips covered with wine
Her dreamy eyes, so totally divine

And when she's kind, it's so very nice
I feel as if I'm in paradise

So, KHUSRO, I'm totally crazy about her
And you know, I'm not her only lover

294 Aey shehsawaar, dast ba soo e inaan mabur

You are the predator and I'm the prey
So come, my love, if only to slay

Your bow and arrow you do not need
You can take my life with a look indeed

Without you, darling, I cannot do
You know, I can never give up on you

So when you kill me, do not throw
My rotting body to a vulture or crow

And come to your KHUSRO without delay
And come, my love, if only to slay

295 Az chashm e to keh hast zay to jaan shikaartar

Come, O my love, and use your dart
And jab, and stab, and wound my heart

And curse me as much as you want
To me it's music, your every taunt

It does not help whatever I do
My silly little heart, it's crazy about you

It would not listen to any advice
However friendly and however nice

It has no patience, no ease, no peace
Its restlessness, oh, it'll never cease

It wants to be always in your street
And whenever possible, to kiss your feet

296 Qamar bureed zay mun mehr o mun kharaab e qamar

Her leaving me, oh, I cannot bear
My night's dark like her raven hair

Her moon-like face is a source of light
And, without her, long and dark is my night

The moon in heaven they hypnotize
My charming moon and her dreamy eyes

And when my moon is shining bright
The sun is shamed, and takes it flight

And when I have the moonlit night
I surely can do without sunlight

That is why, KHUSRO, I cannot bear
When the moon of mine is not there

297 Munam ba khaana, tan een ja o jaan ba jaay diger

My body is here; my soul is there
And my heart, it's only God knows where

For me there's only a lot of grief
From which I cannot find relief

Even when I go to her neighborhood
To me it does not do much good

So when they ask me about her address
I refuse to tell them, I must confess

And when they ask, my heart is where?
I tell them I don't know, it's somewhere there

298 Rukh e gul khush ast o az way rukhat, aey nigaar, khushtar

You're prettier, darling, than any rose
And this, in the garden, everyone knows

So when in the park you aren't there
Even with the flowers, it looks so bare

Of life your mouth is the fountainhead
Your kiss can raise a man from the dead

In the dark of night when I'm alone
I think of you only, and moan and groan

And after I die and go to my grave
For you I'll wait, and pine, and crave

But as of now, I happen to think
I should go to the bar and have a drink

But being your KHUSRO and a faithful slave
For you even there I'll yearn and crave

299 Aey, saram ra ba khaak e paat niaaz

I've now become a slave complete
And love to kiss the dirt of her feet

I feel sometimes great despair
These pangs of love I cannot bear

But even in friends I do not confide
My pains and pangs I try to hide

But then I remember her curly hair
Which makes it even harder to bear

And the more my love I try to forget
The more I miss my Juliet

Then, KHUSRO, her I want to be near
And her voice sweet I want to hear

300 Zay mun chun dil raboodi, raft jaan neez

She stole my soul; she stole my heart
And then very quietly she did depart

O when she speaks, from her sugary lip
Even bitter words like honey drip

I love that juicy, ruby lip
And all its syrup I want to sip

I also want to go to her street
And kiss the dirt of her dainty feet

And in her twisted curly hair
My heart I like as a captive there

And, KHUSRO, though I've a lot of pain
I keep it a secret and never complain

150

301 Kushaadi chashm e khaabaalood ra baaz

O when she looks with those dreamy eyes
She does her lovers all hypnotize

And with those locks on her rosy cheek
She drives these lovers all up the creek

And when in the park she takes a stroll
She makes the birds all trill and troll

And when she wants your poor little heart
She means to break it and take it apart

And when she shoots her deadly dart
She does it to jab and stab your heart

And she can be also cruel and cold
Especially to KHUSRO, her lover old

302 Tan peer gasht o aarzoo e dil jawaan hunooz

Though old I am, my heart is young
And always her name is on my tongue

I worship still that gorgeous dame
Though love for her is only a game

One day, I'm hoping, she'll be mine
When a hope like this looks so asinine

For she's a predator looking for a prey
And a lover she needs only to slay

And while her lover does cry all night
In a comfortable bed she sleeps very tight

And, KHUSRO, though I'm a wounded lover
I'm not a man who's looking for a cover

303   Naazneenaan o chaar baalish e naaz

These beautiful girls, so proud and chic
And all their lovers, so lowly and meek

And although they are so cruel and cold
Somehow on lovers they keep their hold

And while for them they yearn and crave
Their lovers these girls know how to enslave

They think, in love anything is fair
What happens to them, the lovers don't care

It is for the lovers a great pleasure
For love, they think, is a wonderful treasure

And if they feel any pang or pain
They do not tell; they do not complain

And even when, KHUSRO, they want to cry
They all try to keep their eyes dry

304   Bia keh bazm e tarab ra chaman nihaad asaas

Come, O my love, the flowers are here
This is such a beautiful atmosphere

Just bring with you a flask of wine
To quench this terrible thirst of mine

The pangs of love are hard to bear
But I am a lover, I do not care

So pour some wine in a magic bowl
To clean my heart and purge my soul

With a tainted heart, you're always a clown
Even if you don a mystic's gown

And KHUSRO says – just love the Lord
And ignore the punishment and shun the reward

305   Kharaabi e mun az aan chashm e purkhumaari purs

It's a lot of trouble, that dreamy eye
It can stab at will and crucify

Its every lash is like a dart
Which can jab and wound your poor little heart

Beware you also of her bow-like brow
It can kill a hapless lover and how

But though she's cruel, it's also true
That without that gal you cannot do

And though that eye can crucify
It can also soothe and mollify

And although her lover she does mistreat
He loves to kiss the dirt of her feet

So without her, KHUSRO, you're terribly alone
And you sit and cry, and moan, and groan

306   Mara kaarayst mushkil baa dil e khaish

O what do I do with my wayward heart?
Sadly, I know, it's not very smart

It gives me so much sorrow and pain
And I'm not allowed to even complain

And though for it she does not care
It tries to follow her everywhere

And when in chase, it falls behind
It looks for her and cannot find

So when its boat goes upside down
It cannot save it and starts to drown

And then for its wretched, sorry state
It starts to blame its cruel fate

So, KHUSRO, when it'll go to its grave
Even there for her it's going to crave

307 Duzdaana dar aamad az daram doash

She walked last night into my place
With her raven locks covering her face

And when I saw her, I must confess
I almost lost my consciousness

And when I saw that gorgeous face
I was totally dazzled by its beauty and grace

And when she looked, her dreamy eyes
Me, I thought, they will hypnotize

And when I saw that sugary lip
All its honey I wanted to sip

And when she smiled and looked at me
KHUSRO, her slave I wanted to be

308 Saalha khoon khurda am az bakht e baisaamaan e khaish

O since I've been in love with you
My luck has said to me adieu

And now that my heart belongs to you
All sorts of troubles it's getting into

It's at your door all night and day
For away from you it cannot stay

It's now become your slave complete
And wants to kiss the dirt of your feet

For you have lit in it a fire
A fire that's burning its being entire

So your kind attention it surely needs
For without you, darling, it bleeds and bleeds

309 Mast o layaaql guzishtam az dar e maikhaana doash

To have a drink I went to the bar
And saw a mystic sitting not far

Half-drunk was he and half in trance
When he raised his eyes and flashed a glance

The maids of the bar were flirting with men
And the men were happy and saying amen

The candles were also burning very bright
And trying to dispel the dark of night

So after the mystic gave me a glance
He said hello while still in a trance

And asked me to come and sit by him
And fill my cup right up to the brim

And then he whispered this in my ear
"Love you always and love without fear"

310 Doash ma boodaim o jaam e
baada o mehtaab e khush

O drinking and dancing in a moonlit night
With gorgeous girls is a sheer delight

And with their lips all covered with wine
These dames at night look simply divine

Like arches are their beautiful brows
Them worships a lover and to them he bows

And when these dolls do smile and beam
It begins to look a lot like a dream

You start to think it's all an illusion
And finally come to the sad conclusion

That, KHUSRO, it's unlike what it appears
And that life is full of blood and tears

311 Chandeen shabam guzisht ba kunj e kharaab e khaish

My nights are dark without her moon
And keep I hoping that she'll come soon

And when she comes, she'll bring some wine
To quench this terrible thirst of mine

And when she sees me cry and cry
She would want to kiss my tearful eye

Or maybe she would come in my dream
And kiss my mouth before I scream

And when she sees my heart on fire
She would also feel a little desire

So like this, KHUSRO, I cannot stay
I wish she'd come, if only to slay

312 Abr e khush ast o waqt e khush ast o hawa e khush

The spring has come and the flowers are here
So come and bring some wine, my dear

It's softly raining and every flower
Is happily taking in it a shower

This caution of ours O let's forget
And drink and dance, for we may regret

So in this weather we should announce
That drinking and dancing we'll not renounce

Our love and passion we will not control
And to the ones we love we'll give our soul

For all the flowers with all their grace
They cannot compare with a beautiful face

And although in love there's a lot of pain
From it, says KHUSRO, we cannot abstain

313   Aan chashm e sukhangoo nigar o aan lab e khaamoash

Her eyes tell what she does not say
And with her smile she can quickly slay

With a single look she can strike a fire
And burn your heart and soul entire

And with her smile she can also mislead
And make your heart just bleed and bleed

And with those eyes and that charming gaze
She can completely dazzle and she can daze

And with her red, red, rosy cheek
She can make the flowers look all so bleak

And with her locks covering her eyes
She can easily, KHUSRO, mesmerize

314   Geh geh nazaray baaz badaar az mun e durwaish

When come I knocking at your door
I come there only to kiss your floor

Your lips, it's true, I want to kiss
But then you cannot blame me for this

And if I'd like to drink some wine
It's only to dull this reason of mine

For when I adore and worship you
My reason tells me I shouldn't do

But what really drives me up the tree
Is when our KHUSRO starts taunting me

315 Her kas nashista shaad ba kaam o hawa e khaish

They all say loving is a lot of fun
But fun in it I find none

For when it tries and doesn't succeed
My poor little heart, it begins to bleed

And when it fears she's going to leave
Far in advance, it starts to grieve

And knowing well she loves to prey
From her it cannot stay away

And when she wants to clip its wings
It bursts with joy and sings and sings

So, KHUSRO, it seems from all its glee
That it is its own worst enemy

316 Aamad bahaar o shud chaman o laalazaar khush

The spring is happy and the flowers glad
With the trees all green and richly clad

The beautiful maids are so very kind
That teasing and pinching they do not mind

The people are walking and enjoying the breeze
And the lovers are necking under the trees

And in order to boost my low morale
The breeze is bringing the scent of my gal

And with all this love and beauty here
It is such a wonderful atmosphere

And with so much to relish, so much to enjoy
Even KHUSRO is shedding the tears of joy

317   Aey, zay soada e to dar dil ronaq e baazaar e ishq

My heart has lost its sanity
It has now become a sight to see

For the way she uses her charming eye
You can't survive; you simply die

And with her brow, from far away
Without a dart she can easily slay

But even though she loves to kill
She can also cure your every ill

So when the preacher worries about me
Like me, I tell him, he ought to be

And, KHUSRO, though I wail and wail
I tell no one my sorrowful tale

318   Raseed doash nidaay az een buland riwaaq

One night came a heavenly voice
Telling me there is for me a choice

Either to sink in this worldly abyss
Or come and enjoy the heavenly bliss

And leave the world of sin and vice
And live in a place that's clean and nice

Fulfill the promise that was made to God
And do not remain forever a clod

So leave this dungeon, and take this advice
And become a bird of paradise

And listen to KHUSRO; he's a wise guy
He tells the truth and does not lie

319   Turk e sufaid roo o siyehchasm o laalarang

With eyes so dark and face so fair
She's so very chic and debonair

Her raven locks, for better or worse
Have made her the queen of the universe

With a bow-like brow she needs no dart
To jab, and stab, and wound a heart

And for her eyes you are a prey
With a single look they can easily slay

And about her heart, it's also well-known
That her bosom soft does hide a stone

But that her mouth, you know, of course
Of the spring of life it is the source

So, therefore, our KHUSRO, no amateur
Is also very much in love with her

320   Mara behrat khasoomathaast baa dil

This heart of mine is such a pain
It's totally mad, completely insane

Her golden curls have caused my fall
I've been ruined; I've lost my all

I'm also crazy about her eyes
With just a look they so hypnotize

With her I cannot trust my heart
Because I know it's not very smart

It's just a fool, an amateur
From the very start it's stuck on her

And whatever happens, it does not care
It's totally involved in this love affair

For it, she is one and the only one
And like her, KHUSRO, there is none

321 Musalmaanaan baraft az dast e mun dil

I gave my heart to an infidel
But then she's such a beautiful belle

And such a doll that people say
She couldn't have been made from ordinary clay

And so very fair that in the saloon
Everyone thinks she's better than moon

And although her hair is like a snare
Everyone wants to be caught in there

So when I am scolded by a friend
I tell him love he can't comprehend

And if she's always away from me
It is my fate, my destiny

And if they think that I am mad
I don't think, KHUSRO, it's all that bad

322 Khaiz keh jalwa meekunad chehra e dilkusha e gul

With great fanfare the flowers are here
Oh, it's a heavenly atmosphere

The place is bursting with color and scent
And the nightingale seems so content

And like a king of great renown
The rose is sitting, wearing a crown

While the clouds make their thundering sound
And the cypress trees all kiss the ground

And with so much beauty, I'm in a trance
Wanting to sing, and swing, and dance

323 Turk e mun, raftam zay
kooyat ger zay mun gashti malool

She does not want me in her street
For she's afraid I'll kiss her feet

And she won't become my honey bunny
For I've no power; I've no money

So I've to beg the morning breeze
To go to her with all my pleas

While she is there in every part
Of the temple of love, I call my heart

But tell it to the wise I do not dare
Because, KHUSRO, for love they do not care

324 Mun e miskeen cheh kunam,
paish e keh gooyam gham e dil

What is it I've gotten into?
O what do I do; O what do I do?

But then I'm not the only one
This love is a pain to everyone

It doesn't matter how smart you are
In love you cannot go very far

And although there are gals galore
She's the one you love and adore

And if she does not care for you
You can do nothing but do boohoo

325 Rasta boodam, meh e mun, chand geh az zaari e dil

Just when my heart was getting well
I met her again, that beautiful belle

And when she smiled and looked at me
I could not control my ecstasy

A captive it was, my heart, before
But now it's become so even more

Oh, when you love a darling doll
In love you fall and lose it all

In love with her you become a loon
And all your life you cry for the moon

Your cruel fate you cannot defy
So you cry and cry until you die

And, KHUSRO, your fate you curse and curse
And your injured heart you sit and nurse

326 Hamaesha dar firaaqat baa dil e afgaar meegiryam

Oh, how in her absence I'd cry and cry
Although to hide my pain I'd try

And me if she would not like to meet
I'd simply go and cry in her street

I'd moan, and groan, and sigh, and heave
And day and night I'd mourn and grieve

I'd not only cry in the dark of night
But also would weep in the broad daylight

And when it's raining, I'd also cry
Like clouds, O KHUSRO, in the sky

327 Bagooyam haal e khaishat laik az aazaar meetarsam

I will not talk about my pain
Because I do not want to complain

A lovely rose if you want to get
It comes with a thorn; do not forget

So I am living with all this pain
Because I want to see her again

Her eyes dark I love indeed
Because they make my heart so bleed

So please don't laugh if you see me cry
And do not mock my bleeding eye

But even if you are not very kind
Don't worry, KHUSRO, I do not mind

328 Sawaara aamdi o sayd e khud kardi dil o tan hum

She hunts and preys on my heart and soul
My mind, my reason, she wants to control

From her I try to hide my tears
My pain, my sorrow, my dreads, my fears

And when she hits it with her dart
It prays for her, my bleeding heart

And when she wants to chop my head
I bow and tell her to go ahead

And me if a captive she wants to make
I tell her; sure, it's a piece of cake

O she's my moon; I want her light
To brighten the dark of my gloomy night

And she is my goddess; I worship her
For I am, KHUSRO, a faithful lover

329   Soada e sar e zulfat kandar dil o jaan daaram

My pain and sorrow I try to hide
But they're very hard to keep inside

Oh, if that girl I could ever meet
I would rub my eyes over her feet

But love is like a hurricane
And safe in it you cannot remain

And with so much sorrow and so much pain
This love can drive you totally insane

So away from her I cry and cry
And one day, KHUSRO, I'll simply die

330   Jaan zehmat e khud burd o ba jaanaan naraseedaem

Knows she not I'm going to die
And how I sigh and how I cry

A lowly creature, she thinks, I am
For me she does not give a damn

Like dirt I am; I matter not
When for others she cares a lot

For her I'm only a bird of prey
That she can catch and she can slay

So talk I only to the morning breeze
And beg her to go and tell her please

That her I love and her I need
And how my heart does bleed and bleed

331 Umray shud o ma aashiq o diwaana bamaandaem

Though old and weak, I love her still
Knowing my chance is practically nil

A bird I am and a nightingale
My love for flower I cannot curtail

They say I'm old, I should be smart
And I should control my wayward heart

O yes, I'm old but I am a lover
And she's my goddess and I worship her

And her for burning I cannot blame
For I'm the moth and she's the flame

So when I see her beautiful face
I lose my sense of time and space

And, KHUSRO, when I see her hair
I want to be caught in its deadly snare

332 Aashiq shudam o mehram e een kaar nadaaram

This heart is full of pain and grief
And there's no chance of any relief

Yes, things before were also bad
But pain like this I've never had

And though there's so much I want to say
What I feel inside, I cannot convey

My eyes are dark without her light
And day after day I'm losing my sight

All day, all night I cry and cry
And without my gal I'm going to die

My pain and sorrow I try to hide
And to keep it, KHUSRO, all inside

333 Her dam gham e khud ba dil e afgaar bagooyam

Oh, what do I do with all this pain
I cannot show it; I cannot complain

And if I called a spade, a spade
She'll surely scold me, I'm afraid

So if I cannot talk to my doll
I can only go and talk to a wall

I can only yearn, and long, and crave
For I'm a captive, an abject slave

And when they see my terrible plight
Even the heartless feel it's not right

So my love for her I try to hide
But I cannot keep it all inside

And start to hope she will come one night
And herself, KHUSRO, see the blight

334 Babasti chashm e mun zafsoon, zabaan hum

She has my heart, she has my soul
And them with magic she does control

Her dart has wounded me and how
Just ask her eye; go, ask her brow

Kissing her lips O how I miss
O breeze, you go and give her a kiss

O maid of the bar, I'm in a funk
Go bring some wine and make me drunk

You know, I worship a beautiful belle
And people say I'm an infidel

I've lost my creed; I've lost my soul
And KHUSRO thinks I'm in a hole

335 Dil e bai ishq ra mun dil nagooyam

You can't have love without the pain
The pain that makes you go insane

This love is something you can't explain
It has nothing at all to do with brain

And the gal you love has everything
Her mouth is the source of life's spring

So your pain and sorrow you try to bear
And whatever happens, you do not despair

And, KHUSRO, love and follow your heart
And let them say you're not very smart

336 Zaan ghamza e khoonkhaar e jaanafgaar khush meeaayadam

Oh, how her eyes can throw a dart
And jab, and stab, and wound the heart

And you might say it's rather queer
But the wounds of mine I hold very dear

And the way I worship that beautiful belle
You might think I am an infidel

And near the flowers whenever I go
O how I miss her, you do not know

So her if I love and idolize
And for it I'll never apologize

And about her, KHUSRO, I'm going to talk
And talk and talk around the clock

337 Imshab miaan e naukhataan sarmast o ghaltaan booda am

With beautiful gals I sat and drank
And on their kindness yes, I could bank

And I with idols doing so well
For the sheik I was an infidel

And with all these lures around a bloke
Remaining pious was quite a joke

But this was what you saw before
Happy and lively it is no more

Now, KHUSRO, I have nothing but pain
And it has made me quite insane

338 Az ghamza naawakzan shudi, aamaajgaahat dil kunam

Just look at me and use your dart
And jab, and stab, and wound my heart

"Long live", you say, when I die for you
When you know it's something one cannot do

"Cheer up", you say, when I cry and cry
But how can I do it, when you say good-bye?

You prey on me and give me pain
And then you tell me not to complain

And when I want to see your face
You say, "They'll blind you, my beauty and grace"

You then say, "KHUSRO, give me your heart"
When it's already with you, my sweetheart

339 Yak shab ager mun dour az aan gaisoo e darham ooftam

With her raven locks I want to play
And play with them all night and day

Her gorgeous face I want to see
And with her always I want to be

And on her cheek that lovely mole
I love it with my heart and soul

And from her brow when she throws a dart
I want to get it right in my heart

But what I want, I do not get
So, KHUSRO, I curse my fate and fret

340 Aan na munam keh az jafa dast zay yaar dar kasham

O if she's cruel, I do not mind
For the beautiful girls are rarely kind

For there's no rose without a thorn
And without the night here's no morn

But the way she rides her white steed
It shows her birth; it shows her breed

So when she comes in like a gust
I rub in my eyes the flying dust

And when with wine she covers her lip
Oh, how that wine I want to sip

And sip and sip it until I'm drunk
And gotten rid, KHUSRO, of all my funk

341 Aey, khush aan roazay keh ma baa yaar e khud khush booda aem

There was a time when she was mine
And I would kiss her and drink my wine

She was always trying to be with me
And her lovely face I could always see

Using her brow she would throw a dart
That was always meant to hit my heart

Now things have changed and she is gone
And I cry and cry all night till dawn

And KHUSRO is right; love is a fire
And it can consume your being entire

342 Her shabay chun yaad e aan rukhsaar e gulnaari kunam

We talk and talk of her rosy cheek
And tell each other she's so unique

All night long we sigh and sigh
And see our sighs cover the sky

We also talk of her long eyelashes
And how they produce their jabs and slashes

And how they stab and make us bleed
And how much pain it causes indeed

But to KHUSRO, when he sees our pain
We say we love her and cannot complain

343 Saayawaaram her shab az souda e zulfat chun kunam

To my lady dark when I can't get through
With a magic black I try voodoo

But when my patience my pain exceeds
My wounded heart, it bleeds and bleeds

And though she's a predator and I a prey
For her long life I pray and pray

And much like the pearls I shed my tears
And want her to wear them in her ears

But the pangs of love when I cannot bear
I want her to kill me and end my despair

But before she kills me, O KHUSRO my dear
Your verses of love I do want to hear

344 Mun keh dour az doastaan waz yaar dour uftaada am

What happened to her; where did she go?
And where's she now, I do not know?

Everyone is feeling sorry for me
But what can I do with their sympathy?

A stone, I know, I can make it bleed
So why with her do I not succeed?

But I'm not sorry she took my heart
For mind I do not with it to part

But her luscious lips I surly miss
And, KHUSRO, I'm very sure of this

345 Zay to naemat ast o raahat
lab e shakkareen o roo hum

Her cheeks are rosy; her lips are sweet
And her, in flirting, no one can beat

And you might think he's not a lover
But our sheik is also crazy about her

Of showing his love he would not dream
For he is afraid he'll lose esteem

But her gorgeous face whenever he sees
He cannot talk; he starts to freeze

And even our KHUSRO is having an affair
He is also caught in her deadly snare

346 Mun ager bar dar e to her shabay afghan nakunam

I knock at her door and cry and cry
To my self-respect I say good-bye

I'm sure she does not care for it
But wailing, I don't know, how to quit

For a lovely rose whenever I see
Without it, I know, I cannot be

So when people ask me how am I
I just can't help it; I start to cry?

And when they try to help, I say
"O please, O please just go away"

And when KHUSRO asks, I simply exclaim
I cannot help it, I love that dame

347   Soo e mun been keh zay hijrat ba gudaaz amda am

My broken heart has brought me here
Come look at it, O please my dear

See how it loves your curly hair
And how it's caught in its deadly snare

It's also adores your bow-like brow
And the darts it throws it loves and how

Your KHUSRO's heart so come and see
And give it your love and charity

348   Khurram aan roaz keh mun aan rukh e zaiba beenam

Her lovely face I want to see
One day, I hope, she'll come to me

They say her beauty is like the sun
It blinds and dazzles everyone

I know, it will also dazzle me
But I want to see what I cannot see

But if and when she chooses to show
I hope she'll come without my foe

But if she can't, I am so lovelorn
That with my rose I'll take the thorn

Without my gal I feel dismay
And away from her I cannot stay

So, KHUSRO, her I want to meet
If only to kiss her dainty feet

349 Haal e dil baaz bar aaien e digger meebeenam

This love has made me into a clown
It's such a mess, all upside down

My broken heart I sit and nurse
And see things get from bad to worse

She's such a coquette; she's such a flirt
You should see her walk in her tight skirt

You should see her eyes; you should see her brow
For when you'll see them, you'll simply say wow

You should see her mouth and the way she speaks
You should see her nose and her rosy cheeks

And you should see her curly hair
And the way it spreads and flies in the air

And once you see her, KHUSRO my dear
Why I love her will become very clear

350 Gercheh az aql o dil o deeda o jaan bar khaizam

I've lost my heart; I've lost my mind
This love is hard and I'm in a bind

So dying and leaving I would not mind
Because this grind I'll leave behind

I hope my burial she will attend
And feel contrite, or at least pretend

And once in a while come to my tomb
And just for a moment dispel my gloom

And, KHUSRO, I want to say good-bye
I don't want to live and forever cry

351   Aey, ba chashm e to khumaar o khaab hum

Look at those drunken, dreamy eyes
Oh, how they sooth and hypnotize

And look at the curly raven hair
And all those hearts in its deadly snare

And how that face that the tresses shroud
Looks like the moon covered with a cloud

And see you also this tearful eye
When in her absence I cry and cry

And my bleeding heart you should also see
Oh, how it suffers her cruelty

And, KHUSRO, yet being a lover
See how it adores and worships her

352   Aey, rukhat chu maah o az maah baish hum

O she is like the harvest moon
For all her lovers a real boon

And when she throws her deadly darts
They love to get them in their hearts

Without her moon their nights are dark
All very dismal, harsh and stark

So her one night if they do not see
All those lovers are in agony

Her they worship, love and adore
And every day they love her more

And though she gives them great dismay
That live she long, they pray and pray

And whether she's sweet or whether tart
KHUSRO, they think she's a sweetheart

353   Dar firaaqat zindagaani chun kunam

Oh, life is full of pain and grief
And if there's joy, it's only brief

With a heartless girl and cruel fate
You find yourself in a sorry state

And when she leaves, it's even worse
Your broken heart you sit and nurse

And all this sorrow and all this pain
Are enough to drive you totally insane

So life becomes very hard to bear
And if you're poor, you don't have a prayer

And all this, KHUSRO, does make you sick
And your weeping wounds you sit and lick

354   Bar jamaalat mubtalayam, chun kunam

I've fallen in love, what have I done?
I now realize, it's not any fun

To have a doll you must have money
But I have none and that's not funny

O she's a princess meant for a king
And I'm a tramp; I don't have a thing

With her in the park I used to walk
But now to her dog I can only talk

And now in the bar when I go and drink
Of her luscious lips I can only think

So tell me, KHUSRO, what do I do?
I'm so confused; I don't have a clue

355 Az turra e to juz reh e sauda nayaaftam

In the twists and turns of her curly hair
Wherever you look there is a snare

And for my heart when I went to look
There I found it hanging on a hook

And when I saw it caught in there
My pain and sorrow I could not bear

But then I remembered her luscious lip
And the honey from it I used to sip

So there was a time when she was mine
But, KHUSRO, now I can only pine

356 Nay paay aan keh az sar e kooyat safar kunam

In her street I've come to stay
My feelings to her I want to convey

My love to her I want to declare
I cannot wait; I can't forbear

Day and Night I cry and cry
And moan, and groan, and sob, and sigh

All night long I lie awake
Only death can cure my terrible ache

For her I yearn, and pine, and crave
And remain forever her faithful slave

But I also want to tell my story
To anyone who'll listen and for me feel sorry

But, KHUSRO, I do not want any advice
And please don't scold me and just be nice

357   Baa to cheh roaz bood keh mun aashna shudam

Anyone who falls in love with you
To pleasure and joy he says adieu

And when in love he doesn't succeed
His heart and eyes so bleed and bleed

And though he cannot play with your hair
He remains forever in its deadly snare

And then he has to beg the breeze
To take to you his humble pleas

And when people say that he is mad
It makes the fellow feel a lot more sad

And then his sorrow begins to grow
And his love becomes a constant woe

And then he can only yearn and crave
And your KHUSRO becomes an eternal slave

358   Aey deeda, paae sho keh bar e yaar meerawam

To see that gal I went to her street
But me she simply refused to meet

The way of love is a thorny one
With so many troubles, it's no fun

And it's not easy to find your rose
For the way is full of worries and woes

Her gorgeous face you want to see
But to your pleas she wouldn't agree

You want to play with her curly hair
But then you're caught in its deadly snare

So, KHUSRO, then, like a nightingale
What can you do but wail and wail?

359   Ghamam bakusht keh az yaar maanda am, cheh kunam

This love has nothing but sorrow and pain
Her leaving me is inhumane

So weak I am, I can't even cry
And I'm so broken, I want to die

This pain of parting I cannot bear
But my foes are happy to see me despair

But my bleeding eyes when people see
They are as sorry as they can be

And when at night I lie awake
Our KHUSRO thinks that I'm going to break

360   Baraaber e lab e o angbeen chegoona kunam

Red lips she has and a precious nose
And her face looks like a beautiful rose

Her lips are luscious and full of honey
Something you cannot buy with money

In the twists and turns of her curly hair
Wherever you look, you find a snare

So her one day I'd like to meet
And rub my eyes over her feet

And with my tears which are like pearls
I'd like to adorn those precious curls

361 Na yaar waada e boas o kinaar meekunadam

O when she says, "let's sit and neck"
My surge of passion I cannot check

I hope she knows my love for her
And the lust in me that she can stir

So I don't understand when people say
That away from her I should try to stay

But mind I don't when preachers talk
And when they taunt and when they mock

My wine of love I want to drink
And then in a trance I want to sink

And then I want the ecstasy
Of dreaming that, KHUSRO, she belongs to me

362 Zabaan namaand, zay laalat sukhan kuja yaabam

The way I feel, I cannot convey
For what I want, I cannot say

So far you are that even the air
Bring it cannot the scent of your hair

And in the park when you aren't there
For the tulips and roses I do not care

Without you, darling, I cry and cry
And feel as if I'm about to die

I don't mind dying; I'll die for you
You just have to say it and I will do

But I, your KHUSRO, find it scary
The mountain of pain that I've to carry

363 Kidaam sooay rawam kaz firaaq amaam yaabam

My girl is gone; O what do I do?
I'm so lonely; I'm so blue

My life was sunny when she was there
With the sun now gone, it's dark everywhere

The spring of my life has come and gone
My night is dark; I see no dawn

Ever since she left, that beautiful belle
I'm in agony; my life is hell

I've lost my way; I've lost my head
And now it seems I'll soon be dead

But before she shoves me in the abyss
KHUSRO, I want a good-bye kiss

364 Rukhay keh bar cuff e pa e to, seemtan, maalam

If she'd let me kiss her feet
For me it'll be a wonderful treat

And if I could, I certainly would
For I love to stay in her neighborhood

Yes, day and night I think of her
And from our parting I can't recover

For her I long, and yearn, and crave
And this I will carry into my grave

So if I cannot kiss her feet
A failure, KHUSRO, I'll be complete

365 Ghamkashay chand yaar e khaish kunam

Come see my pain and agony
I badly need some sympathy

All night long I wail and wail
And tell my heart my sorry tale

But soon my heart starts to bleed
Which is something I do not need

My pain and sorrow I cannot bear
And caught I am in a deadly snare

Oh, how I suffer and how I ail
But no one wants to hear my tale

May be to KHUSRO I should talk
So at his door I should go and knock

366 Khaiz ta baada dar piyaala kunaem

The spring has come and the flowers are here
Come pour some wine in a cup, my dear

Let's sing and dance and let's not fret
And all the rest let's try to forget

Among the flowers let's sit and dine
And let us drink some ruby wine

I know, you're young and I'm old
But against me this O please don't hold

You ought to see my burning desire
And how the wine can set me on fire

And how your KHUSRO it can immerse
In writing his beautiful, beautiful verse

367 Een toie ta ba khaab meebeenam

Your radiant face is so very bright
It looks like sun shining at night

Your lips are juicy, sweet and red
They are of life the fountainhead

So whenever you go away from me
You leave me in constant agony

But then I'm not the only guy
Whom you torture by saying good-bye

So when you're away, we cannot sleep
And think of your dreamy eyes and weep

368 Az pus e umr shabay humnafas e yaar shudam

She used to herself come to me
But now a dream it appears to be

I'm weak and frail; I sigh and cry
And it surely seems, I'm going to die

But I've found a perfect retreat
I practically live now in her street

Now so much time there I spend
That of her dogs I've become a friend

And it now seems, the way I behave
That I'm her captive, an abject slave

And of my ailment, I am quite sure
That she and only she has the cure

In the meantime, KHUSRO, it seems to me
I have lost all honor, all dignity

369 Dar aa, aey shaakh e gul, khandaan o majlis ra gulistaan kun

Come make it a garden, this lonely heart
O flower of mine, my sweetheart

They say I am an infidel
Because I worship you, my belle

And they won't burry me when I'm dead
They will burn my carcass instead

So come, my goddess, and say good-bye
For see you I must before I die

And you're the doctor who can cure
The pangs of love that I endure

So come and love in my heart renew
And let your KHUSRO worship you

370 Shabay baa ma khayaal e khaishtan ra mehemaan gerdaan

Come please, and with your rosy cheek
Make it a garden, this heart so bleak

And show the flowers your gorgeous face
And make them jealous of your beauty and grace

And with your dark and dreamy eyes
Your lovers all you mesmerize

But when with chains your lovers you bind
Have some pity and try to be kind

And if their blood you have to spill
Use some tact and all your skill

But your face from KHUSRO you must not hide
For he will surely commit suicide

371 Wasiat meekunam ger bashnawad abrookamaan e mun

If you promise to send it through my heart
In my grave I vow to carry your dart

The tongue you speak I don't know at all
So put your tongue in my mouth, my doll

They say your lips are as sweet as honey
But to me they are sweeter, my honey bunny

So even when you do scold me, my dear
It sounds so much like music in my ear

In the fire of love and when I burn
For more of it I yearn and yearn

And KHUSRO knows, when I cry and cry
To reach you, darling, I only try

372 Mubaarak baad maah e roazadaaraan

The month of fasting can also be gay
If you drink at night and doze all day

For when she's fasting, her sleepy eyes
Even the pious they can hypnotize

And when you're thirsty and it does rain
It can relieve you of a lot of pain

You can break your fast with her juicy lips
And sip the nectar while it drips

But do be wary of her long eyelashes
And of their wounding jabs and slashes

And face your love you like a man
And try to sleep whenever you can

And like our KHUSRO drink your wine
With the maid of the bar, for she's divine

373 Bar aamad maah e Eid az auj e gardoon

O it has been sighted, the moon of Eid
And time it is to revel, indeed

We're going to dance, and drink, and eat
And our Romeos and Juliets are going to meet

The sun is setting and the sky is red
And the night its wings will soon spread

And in all its glory, the crescent moon
Will soon be visible from the saloon

And KHUSRO will come and sing his song
And we'll all drink and sing along

374 Khush aamad baa to am deedaar karden

O how I love to see her face
Its bloom and beauty, its charm and grace

For after she drinks a little bit of wine
She looks so pretty, so totally divine

And when she's sleeping in peace and bliss
I love to wake her up with a kiss

With all my heart I love those lips
And sip their nectar as it drips

And being a devoted, faithful lover
I can never stop looking at her

For her I love and her I obey
While me, her prey, she wants to slay

So, KHUSRO, this is my sorry tale
And please forgive me if I wail

375 Aey meer e hama shakarfaroashaan

O queen of beauty, so sugary sweet
You keep your lovers under your feet

Their cries of pain you never heed
You make them cry; you make them bleed

And even a mystic who's a man of God
You somehow make him feel like a clod

And even our sheik who's so very proud
You make him feel just one of the crowd

And their fire of love when it does flare
You do not seem for it to care

And when they cry, and moan, and groan
You simply tell them to leave you alone

And even when KHUSRO dies for you
You shrug and say – it's nothing new

376 Yak dam faraamoasham naie gercheh niaari yaad e mun

My woeful heart you are always near
But what it says, you do not hear

And although you are made of stone
It bothers you when I moan and groan

But when at night I'm in agony
The stars and the moon feel sorry for me

And I'm also grateful to the morning air
For bringing to me the scent of your hair

So I keep telling my broken heart
You'd grin and bear it if you're smart

But when I say there is no hope
Our KHUSRO says I should learn to cope

377 Sauda e khoobaan kum nashud zeen jaan e ghamfarsood e mun

I'm totally crazy about my doll
And have lost my head, my mind, my all

And while I hold her so very dear
She's extremely cruel and insincere

But I surely hope that before I die
She'll come to see me and say good-bye

When people see me, they begin to cry
But she'll be happy to see me die

Although whenever I moan and groan
I can easily melt the heart of a stone

But she wouldn't let me in her street
Even to kiss the dirt of her feet

And tears of blood when I start to shed
She wishes, KHUSRO, that I was dead

378 Maahay guzisht o shab nakhuft een deeda e baidaar e mun

For months I haven't closed my eyes
And I toss and turn until sunrise

And day and night I cry and cry
And people feel I'm going to die

My gal, you know, is a butterfly
May God protect her from the evil eye

My tearful eyes, they make her ill
She gets so mad, she's ready to kill

And I don't mind being killed by her
Because I am such a woeful lover

So I do ask her to kill me please
And finally give me some peace and ease

379 Maah e hilaalabroo e mun, aql e mara shaida makun

Your bow-like brow has hit my heart
With a deadly, deadly, deadly dart

Your raven curls on your rosy cheek
Have made my heart so very, very weak

And the sorrow you have given to me
Is better than the best of gaiety

So come and give me a lot more sorrow
And leave this good work not for tomorrow

I am the moth and you're the flame
So you, for burning, no one can blame

You are my idol, I worship you
And idol-worship is no taboo

And though for KHUSRO it's indiscreet
I love to kiss the dirt of your feet

380 Khaahi dila firdous e jaan, rukhsaar e jaanaan ra babeen

Her cheeks have roses, you will agree
And she's tall and slim like a cypress tree

And in my heart I have a fire
That can consume the world entire

She gets so angry whenever I cry
That me she'd like to crucify

And when she goes into a fury
She looks prettier than a heavenly houri

But when she is very calm and serene
She's every bit, KHUSRO, a divine queen

381 Gercheh zay khoo e nazukat
soakhta gasht jaan e mun

In the fire of love I'm burning, my dear
My pain has never been quite so severe

With so much pain and when I weep
People who see me, they cannot sleep

Away from you oh, how I suffer
And the problem I have cannot be tougher

So without you, darling, I will go bust
And soon will become a handful of dust

But luckily we have a righteous king
To whom our troubles we all can bring

To the meek and weak he is a friend
And on his kindness we can always depend

And though he's busy as anyone can be
For his poor KHUSRO he's never too busy

382 Rafti o shud bai to jaanam zaar, baaz aa o babeen

Come see how weak and frail I am
And without you how I'm in a jam

I look for you and wait and wait
Do come and see my sorry state

I am thin and feeble as I can be
This pain of parting is killing me

And I feel sure I'm about to die
So come if only to say good-bye

I'm dying to play with your curly hair
And stroke my heart that's caught in there

So if you like a lover insane
Come then and see your KHUSRO in pain

383   Subh e doulat meedamad ya khud rukh e jaanaast een

Her radiant face is like the sun
Her cheeks are rosy; like her is none

Her eyes are dark, her lips maroon
And she is golden like the moon

So when people see her gorgeous face
They see in it the divine grace

But loving that gal is a lot of pain
Your tears, they fall like the rain

So then you go to our valiant king
And to his feet you want to cling

And beg him to take you under his wing
And, like our KHUSRO, his praise you sing

384   Aey, ba kooyat her sahargeh jaa e tanhamaandgaan

Your lovers all are in your street
Weeping but trying to be discreet

And when their blood, your place it smears
They try to wash it with so many tears

To see your face they wait and wait
Just come and see their sorry state

Without you nights are bleak and stark
So all night long they grope in the dark

And without you also they feel very lonely
For they love you only; they love you only

So come and see the great despair
Especially of KHUSRO who is also there

385   Chasm ra dar mulk e khoobi shehna e baidaad kun

Her cruel eyes, they'll wound your heart
It'll go through you, their every dart

And be you aware of her curly hair
For she'll trap you in its deadly snare

She'll look at you with her dreamy eyes
Only to charm you and mesmerize

And soon you'll feel like an amateur
Unable to hide your love for her

You'll always want to see her face
And will look for it from place to place

And soon she'll be in complete control
Able to hurt or soothe your soul

She'll make you dance on her every tune
And even our KHUSRO will not be immune

386   Aey dil, ba chashm e ibrat nazzaara e jahaan kun

O look at things the way they are
And what you want, it won't be far

To the seventh heaven you can surely go
And the mystery of being you can also know

And if you're good and not too clever
You can be immortal and live for ever

And if you can give up what you own
You can be fit to sit on a throne

And if you want to see the light
A fire in your soul you must ignite

And you can surely become a king
If like KHUSRO you can write and sing

387 Aey, baikhabar zay deeda e baikhaab e aashiqaan

Your lovers all, they cannot sleep
In the fire of love they burn and weep

And about you when they start to talk
They talk and talk around the clock

And though not sleeping, dream they do
But then they can only dream about you

And when their hearts begin to bleed
Your urgent attention oh, how they need

And KHUSRO, when he sees their plight
He prays for them and cries all night

388 Jaana, shabay ba koo e ghareebaan muqaam kun

O come one day your lovers to meet
And see how they all kiss your feet

And if complain to you they dare
Their broken hearts do try to repair

And about the preacher if they complain
You should assure them that he is insane

Look how they love your dreamy eyes
And see how them they hypnotize

And how they adore even your dog
And how they listen to his monologue

Without you they all feel very blue
They yearn, and crave, and lust for you

But when KHUSRO says they should forbear
They all get mad and start to swear

389 Sawaab neest ba to fikr e hoor e ein karden

Her brow is like the crescent moon
Her curls are black, her lips maroon

But like I not a bit when she
Becomes so friendly to my enemy

And sadly him she does prefer
Over me who's willing to die for her

So all this tells me to go to the bar
And there I empty the wine jar

But then this makes me terribly miss
KHUSRO, the lips that I crave to kiss

390 Chuneen keh bai to zamaanay nameetawaan boodan

I cannot bear parting with you
Without you, darling, I cannot do

Yes, I'm a tramp and you a queen
And you, I know, I do demean

But my tears are like the precious pearls
And these you can use in your golden curls

You say that I should forget about you
But this, you know, I can never do

And against you, dear, I cannot hold
If you are so cruel, callous and cold

So please, for God's sake, don't get upset
If you your KHUSRO cannot forget

391 Aalam az jaam e lab kharaab makun

O it's your lips and not the wine
For which I yearn, and crave, and pine

And it's your face and not the moon
For my nights dark that is the boon

And it's in the night lit by your face
That my woeful heart for robbing you case

And it's your curl and not the chain
With which you bind me again and again

And it's crying for you night after night
That's taken away from my eyes the light

So come, my darling, and with your face
Light up your KHUSRO'S dingy place

392 Hameeraizi ba baazi khoon e yaaraan

Killing for her is just a game
But then she is a beautiful dame

And I'm a lover who people mock
And have now made me a laughingstock

I'm old, and tired, and sad, and blue
And she's as fresh as the morning dew

My heart is weak; it bleeds and bleeds
And help from her oh, how it needs

Oh, how I suffer and how I ail
And no one is there to hear my tale

So KHUSRO, I am a nightingale
Who now does nothing but wail and wail

393 Yak shab, aey maah e jahaanafroaz e mun

O, come one night, my gorgeous moon
To make it bright and do it soon

Oh, in my heart there is a fire
That is consuming my being entire

And yet my nights are cold and dark
And there's no light, not even a spark

And then this preacher, he makes me sick
Because on me he loves to pick

So I, your KHUSRO, then cry and cry
And moan, and groan, and sob, and sigh

394 Imroaz ba nazzaara e aan sarv e kharaamaan

When sheiks and preachers saw my doll
They couldn't help feeling all very small

They lost their hearts; they lost their creed
They lost whatever they had indeed

And stopped they caring for their name
Her abject slaves and they all became

And after they saw her raven curls
They stopped looking at the other girls

And after they smelt the scent of her hair
They all got trapped in her deadly snare

And then they knew why KHUSRO had pain
And why he'd become so totally insane

395   Dilam ra kard sadpaara ba seena khaarkhaar e to

This pain is breaking my poor little heart
It's terribly wounded; it's falling apart

Yes, at her door I'm banging my head
And will not stop until I am dead

O how I wish she'd open the door
And hear me out and not ignore

Well, I'm the moth and she the flame
So her for burning me I will not blame

And I won't mind her wounding my heart
As long as she does it by using her dart

And I will bleed and very gladly die
If, KHUSRO, she kills me with her dreamy eye

396   Dilam aashufta shud, jaana, ba baala e bala e to

O what is this I have gotten into
And why am I so involved in you?

I know you're cruel, callous and cold
And yet on me you've such a hold

But I love the way you lure and flirt
And the way you walk in your tight skirt

And I also love to see your face
With all its beauty, charm and grace

But why are you nice to everyone
And only your KHUSRO you always shun?

397   Baichaara dilam khoon shud dar paish e khayaal e to

My poor little heart, it bleeds and bleeds
Her kind attention oh, how it needs

I've lost my mind; I've lost my soul
And having lost my all, I'm in a hole

For since I've seen her beautiful face
I've surely become a very sad case

Everything it has I love a lot
Its blush, its dimple, its beauty spot

But then I'm not her only lover
Everyone, I know, is crazy about her

Even KHUSRO, they say, is in bad shape
Her charm and beauty he too can't escape

398   Aey, jaan e mun aawaizaan az band e qaba e to

Oh, how I love the way you flirt
And the way you walk in your tight skirt

And when I see you in your street
I want to kiss the dirt of your feet

But then it's also because of you
That I cry, and sigh, and do boohoo

And the fire of love when burns it bright
I cannot sleep a wink all night

But then I begin to wish and pray
That come you will, if only to slay

And though I'm KHUSRO, the king of verse
I feel as if I'm your slave or worse

399 Khalqay hama dar shehr o mara ja ba digger soo

They go their way and I go mine
And I get clobbered and they do fine

And her one day if I happen to meet
I can't even dare to kiss her feet

And then when she says to me good-bye
I can only grieve and cry and cry

I cry so much, I lose my mind
And look for her but cannot find

And then I yearn, and crave, and pine
Knowing she'll never again be mine

But there was a time that we were close
Just like a nightingale and a rose

But all this, KHUSRO, is dead and gone
It's now only something to brood upon

400 Zeen saan keh naawak meezanad chashm e shikaarandaaz e o

Her eyes when they throw their darts
Become their prey the bravest of hearts

And her raven curls when they trap and snare
Even sheiks and preachers don't have a prayer

And when she captures even a sage
Forever she keeps him safe in a cage

And when that siren sings her song
Whoever hears it, he sings along

And even our KHUSRO becomes a buffoon
And day and night he cries for the moon

401   Gercheh keh hast khoon e dil baada e khushgawaar e to

The blood of lovers, her eyes think
Is like the wine for them to drink

But their drinking blood the lovers don't mind
If she'd only come and just be kind

And when she hunts, they say hurrah
And fiercely compete to be her prey

But if she comes not, they sit in the street
Wanting to kiss the dirt of her feet

And in this quest if they do not succeed
Form their broken hearts they bleed and bleed

They moan, and groan, and sob, and sigh
And without her, KHUSRO, they all want to die

402   Baaz ba khoon e khalq shud chashm e jafanuma e to

They make it bleed, those cruel eyes
Oh, how this heart they penalize

In love with her, I've had no luck
I'm completely caught, so badly stuck

But though she makes my life hell
I pray for her and wish her well

I also pray that when we meet
She'll kindly let me kiss her feet

And then she'll ask me to sing a song
And, KHUSRO, she'll also sing along

403 Mast meegardi zay khaana, baish naafarmaan mashoo

O don't go out when you are high
Beware, my love, of the evil eye

You are the gal they all want to woo
And they're so willing to die for you

But you take their hearts and throw them away
And care you not if you cause dismay

You also like to throw them bait
And those who take it, you devastate

But then sometimes when you apologize
It comes to KHUSRO as a great surprise

404 Her shab munam uftaada ba gird e sara e to

Around your house I walk all night
And cry and cry until daylight

And though old and weak and falling apart
I love you still with all my heart

I know for sure you'll never be mine
But to this, my love, I'll never resign

That's why I go and sit in your street
And whenever I can, I kiss your feet

So please on KHUSRO some pity take
He's your slave; do give him a break

405 Ta shudam chashmaashna baa roo e to

Ever since, my love, I've seen your face
Everything with me is out of place

You cheek is like the rosy wine
In which I see the image divine

A beautiful rose and when I smell
I smell in it your scent, my belle

And a rainbow when I see in the sky
"Oh, it is her brow", I start to cry

So when you're away, I weep and weep
And seeing me weeping, no one can sleep

I wish you'll come and see this blight
And decide to kiss me and hold me tight

406 Dilay daaram chu daamaan e gul az gham chaak gerdeeda

My poor little heart, it's falling apart
And also my prudence, it's about to depart

These pangs and pains I cannot bear
I'm ripping my clothes; I'm tearing my hair

And I am in such an agony
That everyone is feeling sorry for me

But, you know, she's a very beautiful dame
And her for my pain I cannot blame

But I do wish, KHUSRO, she'd come one day
And kindly hear what I have to say

407   Dilay daaram zay hijraan paara, paara

From her eye she throws a dart
That does go right through your heart

And when she reveals her gorgeous face
You fall in love with its beauty and grace

But then she can also cause despair
And you rip your clothes and tear your hair

And she can give you so much pain
That it will drive you totally insane

And she is also an infidel
And will lead you straight to hell

Even so, KHUSRO, you will never miss
A chance her luscious lips to kiss

408   Dilam dar ishq e jaanaan gashta paara

My loving heart is falling apart
And she has such a stony heart

My eyes are shedding such tears of blood
That soon, I'm afraid, there will be a flood

And as I cry, I think of her lip
From which red wine I used to sip

But my friends all tell me not to cry
For they're afraid I'm going to die

My broken heart they want to repair
But know they not my great despair

For to that dame I'm a little boy
And, KHUSRO, my heart merely a toy

409 Naseem e zulf bar dast e saba deh

O while I am in its deadly snare
You let my rival play with your hair

And while you are so nice to him
I find you always grumpy and grim

And if with you I want to be
You simply refuse to be with me

I wish you will end this agony
And kill me and be finished with me

Or burn me down and throw the ash
Wherever you find a heap of trash

But please do something about this pain
For it is driving your KHUSRO insane

410 Aey, aarzoo e hazaar seena

They love you and they lust for you
But care you do not what they do

For you they sob, and sigh, and cry
Their doleful eyes are never dry

On them advice has no effect
For reason and caution they simply reject

They shout, they love you, again and again
It seems they've become completely insane

And even our KHUSRO, who is so cool
He does now also behaves like a fool

411 Ger kuni gasht e chaman baa shoukh o baa shangay do seh

It's nice to be in the park with girls
And smell the locks and play with curls

And try to look into their eyes
While they enchant and mesmerize

And tell them how you love their lips
Their necks and shoulders, their waists and hips

And if they resist and start to fight
Try to be gentle but hold them tight

And if they are stony hard and cold
Be not discouraged and try to be bold

And listen to KHUSRO and lose not heart
Even if you find them cruel and tart

412 Meh e mun, kharaab gashtam zay rukhat ba yak nazaara

O her enchanting, dreamy eyes
They intoxicate; they hypnotize

And O her glowing, gorgeous face
They dazzle you, its beauty and grace

And it's so brilliant; it's so bright
That a million eyes from it get light

And when in the park she takes a walk
Everyone starts to ogle and gawk

And, KHUSRO, when she breaks a heart
It not only breaks, it falls apart

413   Aey, tura jour o jafa aaien hama

Oh, why are you so very cruel and cold?
And why on me you've such a hold?

And why to my foe you're so very kind
When, you know, he has such a filthy mind?

To me you're always grumpy and grim
But somehow you always favor him

I know, my love, you are the queen
And you by loving I do demean

And when they see your gorgeous face
The tulips and roses feel so commonplace

So it's no wonder you're cruel and cold
And on your KHUSRO you have such a hold

414   Shum e falak bar aayad baa aatisheen zabaana

O it's a beautiful moonlit night
Let's all drink and let's get tight

It's time to have some ruby wine
Let's go to the bar and quit this shrine

Let's also ask my gal to come
For without her life is sad and glum

I want her to come and be with me
And join me in my drinking spree

And since it's also the time of spring
A song of love I want her to sing

Then, KHUSRO, I want her to go in a trance
And with me all night to dance and dance

415   Bia shabay bar e mun sarkhush az sharaab shuda

O come to me and bring some wine
It needs your help, this heart of mine

And when you come, don't use the lace
Of your locks and curls to hide your face

O I don't mind if you're not sincere
For I'm accustomed to it, my dear

Your love, my love, has made me a loon
For in beauty and grace you're better than moon

So come to your KHUSRO, this poor guy
He loves you so; don't let him cry

416   Aey, firaaq e to yaar e daerina

Her absence, you know, is nothing new
And also this pain I'm getting used to

These pangs of love don't bother me
I know from them I'll never be free

Oh, people drink and people dance
But I can't even go into a trance

In the fire of love I burn and burn
I long and pine; I crave and yearn

I wish one day the breeze will go
And tell my gal that I love her so

But I can't help feeling it's no use
It's all my fault; I've no excuse

And, KHUSRO, since I've seen that doll
I feel I am up against the wall

417 Dar ausaaf e khud aql ra reh madeh

O love has nothing to do with brain
For it's something you cannot explain

All men are crazy about their girls
They simply adore those fragrant curls

But the lovers have also a lot of pain
For the beautiful girls are not humane

And when their lovers all sigh and cry
These gorgeous girls don't ever ask why?

So, KHUSRO, in love you live with woe
For being a lover you cannot say no

418 Ba girdat baad e sarday her dam az ushshaaq e deewaana

Her crazy lovers, they tear their hair
Her raven curls when they fly in the air

Her beautiful face and when they see
They're in so much trouble, they all agree

And when they see her dreamy eyes
They all are afraid they cannot survive

And the flowers without her when they bloom
They see in the garden nothing but gloom

And in the bar when she is not there
In the cups and pitchers they all see despair

And when she comes to hunt and prey
They want to be slayed without delay

"Do burn us please", they all exclaim
For they are the moths and she the flame

And about her KHUSRO, when he starts to talk
They beg him to talk around the clock

419   Aey dard e baidard e dilam, taaraaj e pinhaan kardaie

You took my heart and gave me grief
Now kill me and give me a little relief

And after you've made my life hell
I don't know how you can sleep so well

I wish you'd tell your cruel eyes
My poor little heart not to victimize

You can hurt a heart and make it weep
A lover's heart, you think, is cheap

I know that you are a beautiful flower
And the nightingales are all in your power

And you are a gal they all want to woo
And even KHUSRO cries all night for you

420   Seena am ra az gham e aalam to baigham karda ie

Worrying about you is a full time job
All day, all night I sigh and sob

They all feel sorry when they see me cry
But you never do; I don't know why?

And instead of showing me some sympathy
You make my life very hard for me

And when you can, you use the art
With long eyelashes of wounding a heart

And you also use your KHUSRO's tears
As rubies and pearls, to adorn your ears

421 Aey, keh dar heetch ghamay baa dil e mun yaar na ie

She cares for no one, that cruel dame
For love for her is only a game

My loving that gal is nothing new
But why do I do it, I don't have a clue

And no one sleeps when I cry at night
Except for her; she sleeps so tight

Lovesick I am; I need a kiss
Her red, red lips oh, how I miss

And need I someone who'd listen to me
And give me, KHUSRO, some sympathy

422 Deedi keh haq e khidmat e bisyaar na deedi

Known she has not sorrow and pain
That's why she has so much disdain

And that's why she is cruel and cold
And cares she not for her lover old

Like a proud goddess she stand above
And knows she not what's it to love

And why should she pity a lover's plight
When known she has not a sleepless night?

And KHUSRO my friend, why should she care
When God's made her the fairest of fair?

423 Chuneen kaan khanda e sheereen to kardi

Oh, on her lips that lovely smile
It does enchant; it does beguile

And when she puckers those lips of hers
Your lust and desire oh, how she stirs

Without your knowing she steals your heart
Only to break it and take it apart

And she likes to break it again and again
No matter how much it gives you pain

And also she is a godless belle
Who can make a sheik an infidel

And even our KHUSRO is not immune
For she can make him act like a loon

424 Nay kaar e kasayst ishqbaazi

In love you either make or break
Your life is always at the stake

And if your life you do not lose
You'll have nothing except the blues

A miserable life you're going to lead
Your poor little heart, it'll bleed and bleed

And even if you are a mighty king
You'll lose your realm and everything

You'll lose your faith; you'll lose your creed
An infidel you will become indeed

And you will yearn and you will crave
And, KHUSRO, you will become a slave

425   Neest dilay keh her damash aafat e deen nameeshawi

There isn't a lover she hasn't hurt
That great coquette, that gorgeous flirt

Everyone knows she's cruel and cold
And there's no torture she does withhold

But when she shines in her saloon
In grace and beauty she shames the moon

So I hope one day she'll come to my room
And dispel her KHUSRO's deadly gloom

426   Baaz behr e jaan e ma ra naaz dar sar meekuni

It's we lovers who've made her so proud
But why did we do it, for crying out loud?

And because her favors we always seek
She has made us all so frail and weak

And because we love her with heart and soul
We have driven ourselves all into a hole

And because she's also an infidel
One day we all will be going to hell

And, KHUSRO, she's made us even try voodoo
But her there was no way we could possibly woo

427 Zay nazar agercheh douri, shab o roaz dar huzoori

All day, all night I cry for you
Without you, darling, I cannot do

Your absence, love, I cannot bear
This being alone is a nightmare

I know, your beauty has made you cold
And care you not for this lover old

But I also know that you can be nice
And convert this hell into paradise

My tearful eyes so come and see
They need your pity, your sympathy

And see how dark's your KHUSRO's night
And how very badly it needs your light

428 Aey baigham az dil e mun, bisyaar shud judaaie

Why do I miss you so much, my doll
When care you do not for me at all?

You can't even picture my terrible plight
When known you've never a sleepless night

About me people now talk and talk
This love has made me a laughingstock

And it fills them all with great disgust
When they see me treated like a speck of dust

Only KHUSRO, however, is nice to me
For only he understands my tragedy

429   Aan keh jaan gooyand khalqay, aan toie

O you are my life; you are my soul
My total purpose, my only goal

I may be base; I may be mean
But you I worship, my glorious queen

You are my ruler; you own my heart
And control you also its every part

But since in it you have a stake
This poor little heart O please don't break

And do not give me sorrow and pain
For I'm your KHUSRO, simple and plain

430   Salaam o khidmat e ma, aey saba, ba yaar bagoo

Go you, O breeze, and tell her hi
And tell her how I cry and cry

And try to make that girl aware
That I cannot wait; I cannot forbear

And tell her about my sorrow and pain
And how they're driving me insane

And if that gal has forgotten me
Try to tell her how it used to be

And how I used to sigh and cry
Whenever she said to me good-bye

And how I used to yearn and crave
And how KHUSRO thought I was her slave

431 Heetch shakkar chu aan dahaan deedi

Her lips are juicy, sweet and red
Her mouth is life's fountainhead

And she is a rose for whom I wail
Night and day like a nightingale

And she is like a cypress tree
With all its grace and dignity

And every night in her saloon
In charm and beauty she shames the moon

And even our KHUSRO, no amateur
Is madly, madly in love with her

432 Mara doash gooie ba khaab aamdi

Last night she came with a cup in hand
Sipping the wine and looking so grand

And when she smiled, I forgot my funk
Just seeing her dinking did make me drunk

It also set my heart on fire
With love and lust and burning desire

And suddenly my dark and dingy night
Became all bright with her moonlight

And, KHUSRO, when I saw her moon
I started to behave like a loon

433 Taa daasht ba jaan taaqat, boodam ba shakaibaaie

Once my heart was strong and sure
Much pain and sorrow it could endure

But now it has lost its old flair
And the slightest sorrow it cannot bear

Now things are totally out of control
The pain of her parting has taken its toll

And when I say she ought to care
She simply tell me, I must forbear

And when I tell her, it makes me sad
She laughs and says I'm completely mad

I guess she's right, I am insane
Because, KHUSRO, I cry so much in vain

434 Dila, aan Turk ra deedi, kunoon saamaan kuja beeni

If ever, friends, you went to her street
All kinds of lovers you're going to meet

And when she rides her white steed
She ends up causing a stampede

Everybody wants to be with her
But favors she not a single lover

So then they all sit around her house
And fuss, and grumble, and grunt, and grouse

She gets so mad, she wants to kill
For her lovers' blood she loves to spill

And when she hears their cries of pain
KHUSRO, she thinks they are all insane

435 Gahay banmaa o geh
poasheeda daar aan roo e gulnaari

Oh, when she hides behind the veil
Her lovers all so wail and wail

But when her face she wants to show
These woeful lovers, they start to glow

Of kissing that face they start to dream
And this very thought does make them scream

But she being cruel, callous and cold
She gets very upset and starts to scold

But all this cruelty they do not mind
Because their love is totally blind

She is their goddess; she's their queen
And all this they take it to be routine

These lovers are hardy as they can be
But they still need, KHUSRO, some sympathy

436 Dilam keh laaf zaday az kamaal e daanaaie

There was a time when I had a heart
That used to say it was so smart

With someone's parting it could easily deal
And alone and lonely it never did feel

It would be happy with the morning air
If it could bring the scent of her hair

But now this heart has said good-bye
It wants to live with a cutie pie

It sounds so like an amateur
And says it's madly in love with her

And, KHUSRO, it loves her curly hair
And does not mind its deadly snare

437 To, aey pisar, keh az een soo sawaar meeguzri

Riding whenever she comes this way
She comes here only to hunt and prey

And though she used to see me a lot
She now pretends she knows me not

O she's a rose, but with her scorn
She can hurt me much like a thorn

And cares she not for my terrible plight
For known she has never a sleepless night

And knows she not how to sympathize
And what does it matter if her KHUSRO cries?

438 Badeen sifat keh babasti kamar ba khoonkhaari

It's her right to hunt and prey
It's her custom; it's her way

Her lovers also, they do not mind
If she is cruel and not very kind

They do not mind if she is curt
And when she hurts them, it doesn't hurt

They don't mind if they have to weep
And all night long if they cannot sleep

In short, O KHUSRO, they like to cry
And for their gal they all want to die

439 Ba khoobi humchu meh taabinda baashi

Come rise and shine like the moon
Your lovers are waiting in the saloon

And look at them with dreamy eyes
And charm them all and mesmerize

And don't be cruel to them, my pet
And don't do anything that you'll regret

So come and charm them with your smile
And make their lives a little worthwhile

For when you're angry, it makes them sad
And when you're laughing, they are all very glad

440 Aey, kaash mara baa to sarokaar na booday

I wish I did not meet that doll
In love with her and I did not fall

For if those curls I did not see
Today her captive I would not be

And If I did not see those eyes
I would not be acting so unwise

And if her favor I did not seek
I wouldn't be so very frail and weak

And, KHUSRO, if I were a little smart
I wouldn't be nursing this broken heart

441 Saba zulf e tura ger dam na daaday

Her curls, if they did not fly in the breeze
We all wouldn't have lost our peace and ease

And if she did not twist her hair
We all wouldn't have been in such despair

And if there were no love and desire
We wouldn't have been in a state so dire

And if we lovers were a little smart
Our hearts wouldn't have been falling apart

So, KHUSRO, if we didn't love her hair
Today we wouldn't have been in this snare

442 Paish az een mun baa jawaanaan aashnaaie kardamay

I fell in love with a lovely lass
Only to fall in a deep morass

At first it made me extremely glad
For it gave me something I never had

And when that gal spoke to me
It sounded so like a rhapsody

But soon there came the parting pain
A pain that made me totally insane

And living without that beautiful belle
Became for me a veritable hell

So then I started to wail and wail
Which made me, KHUSRO, a nightingale

443   Doash meeguft peer e tarsaay

The keeper of the bar was saying last night
And what he said was completely right

He said if you want a friendly club
You ought to go to your neighborhood pub

Here topers sing, and drink, and dance
And you should see when they go in a trance

They shout her name again and again
It looks as if they're totally insane

And about the houris when the preacher talks
They can only think of their baby's locks

They can also see her bringing the wine
And flirting with them and looking divine

So that's what happens when you love someone
And, KHUSRO, this can happen to anyone

444   Na bood yaar e mun, aan ra keh yaar daashtamay

There is no gal like my gal
O she's my darling; she is my pal

She gives me, however, a lot of woe
Although she tells me I am her beau

And she also likes to use her dart
To jab, and stab, and wound my heart

She makes me sob, and sigh, and cry
So that my eyes are never dry

And although she is very, very sweet
She wouldn't let me kiss even her feet

Yet she's my gal and I her guy
And, KHUSRO, for her I'm ready to die

KHUSRO
HAFIZ
GHALIB
& FAIZ

Read Free

English and Urdu translation in VERSE of the Persian poems of

KHUSRO and HAFIZ

and

English translation in VERSE of the Urdu poems of GHALIB and FAIZ

by

Logging on to URL: www.writing.com/authors/khalmeed

Searching through Google under: Khalid Hameed Shaida

Buy Paper, Audio and E Books

FROM www.amazon.com and other etailers
1.   Khusro, the Indian Orpheus, a hundred odes
2.   Amir Khusro, The Nightingale of India, Selected Persian Odes
3.   Hafiz, the Voice of God, a hundred odes
4.   Hafiz, Drunk with God, selected odes
5.   Ghalib, the Indian Beloved, Urdu odes
6.   Faiz, a Wailing Nightingale, Urdu poems

Buy Paper Books

FROM Suraj, 6/A Naseeruddin Road,
Islampura, Lahore, Pakistan.
Email: surajquarterly@yahoo.com
1. Dr. Khalid Hameed Shaida Number I with English and Urdu Translation
of Ghalib
2. Dr. Khalid Hameed Shaida Number II with English and Urdu Translation
of Hafiz
3. Khusro aur Iqbal with English and Urdu Translation of Khusro and Iqbal

Write to the translator:
Khalid Hameed Shaida, MD

2208 Lakeway Drive, Friendswood, TX 77546, USA Email: khalmeed@aol.com

Made in the USA
Las Vegas, NV
28 May 2024